Scrapbooking Made Easy!

Jill A. Rinner

TIME
LIFE
BOOKS

Alexandria, Virginia

Time-Life Books is a division of Time Life Inc.

TIME LIFE INC.
PRESIDENT AND CEO: George Artandi
EXECUTIVE VICE PRESIDENT: Lawrence J. Marmon

TIME-LIFE CUSTOM PUBLISHING
VICE PRESIDENT AND PUBLISHER: Terry Newell
VICE PRESIDENT OF SALES AND MARKETING: Neil Levin
Director of Acquisitions and Editorial Resources: Jennifer Pearce
Editor: Linda Bellamy
Director of Creative Services: Laura McNeill
Technical Specialist: Monika Lynde
Production Manager: Carolyn Bounds
Quality Assurance Manager: James D. King

First printing. Printed in U.S.A.
Pre-Press Services, Time-Life Imaging Center

Library of Congress Cataloging-in-Publication Data
Rinner, Jill A.
    Scrapbooking Made Easy! / Jill A. Rinner.
        p. cm.
    Includes index.
    ISBN 0-7370-0058-9
    1. Photograph albums. 2. Photographs--Conservation and restoration.
  3. Scrapbooks. I. Title.
    TR465.R55 1999
    745.593--dc21
                                                    99-38593
                                                      CIP

Contents

A Note from the Author

THINK FOR A MINUTE about a wonderful memory you have made with your family and friends. It might be of a child's birth, a wonderful vacation, or any number of everyday activities that make our lives meaningful. If prompted, how many others could remember the details to such an event? If photographs were taken of this event, have you looked at them since having them developed? Is this an event that was important enough that you would want to share it with others?

This book has been designed to help you record those cherished memories in a creative way. This is not just a how-to book. It is not about projects that I have created that you should copy. That would only make your scrapbook pages a documentation of my personality and life. This book is designed to teach you to make scrapbook pages that are about YOU! Scrapbooks are no longer just about pictures pasted onto paper. They are about recording those moments that have been meaningful to you and your family. This can be done in a creative and fun way that will keep the memories alive forever. Scrapbooks can be a window into your soul.

This book has been organized into eight sections, with each one focusing on an essential topic. The first section will start you out on those guidelines that are important to know before beginning on the scrapbooking adventure. If you have already begun your journey, then the following sections will teach you the principles of the creative process associated with recording this unique personal history. These sections do not have to be read in order. Skip around to the sections to learn more about these topics as you need them. This book will become your ultimate guide for inspiration and education.

Whether you are a beginner, intermediate or advanced scrapbook artist, this book will help you draw on your own creative instincts or help you to gain that creativity. As you understand the concepts of design, color, journaling and so forth, you will then be able to draw upon those cherished memories to create scrapbook pages that are truly an expression of you. A scrapbook is meant to be a personal creation of your life's journey.

The samples that you will see in this book are from my life's journey. They were not made as generic samples for this publication. They are from real memories I have made with my family and friends. I would like to share them with you as a means to show you how you can learn to express yourself through artistic creation and can document your life so your family who comes after you may know you. I am propping open the window to my soul and allowing you a peak inside, in hope that you will be touched by the possibilities that lie in front of you, the possibilities of wonderful scrapbook pages that will house your history. May you have a fabulous time as you embark on this journey of keeping your memories alive!

—Jill A. Rinner

Things You Should Know

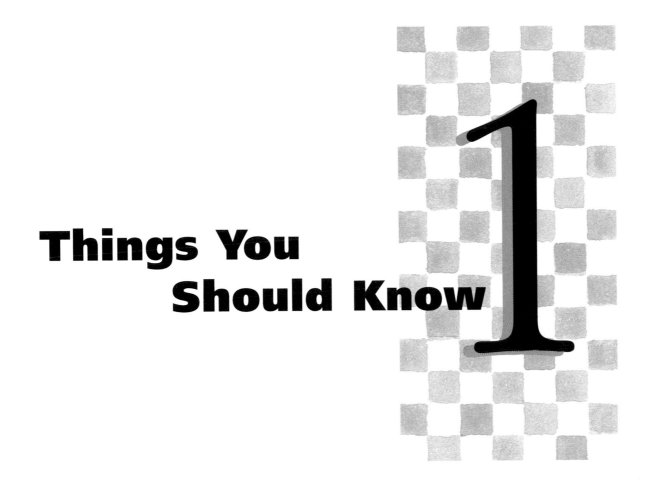

IF YOUR LIFE IS ANYTHING LIKE MINE, YOU are always looking for ways to make things easier. There are always things to be done that keep me from doing the one thing I want to do most: scrapbook my memories. In this chapter, I will share with you the things you should know to help you understand how meaningful yet simple preserving your memories can be. The market for scrapbooking materials has rapidly grown, particularly in the last few years, and there is much to be learned of this new "art."

Information equals education, and when you are informed, you will be able to make decisions to protect your photos and memories in the best possible way!

protecting your photos

There are some things in life that seem obvious, things your mother probably told you when you were little: don't touch fire, look both ways before crossing the street, and keep your photos protected and organized. Oh, did your mother forget to throw that last one in? I know mine did, even though she had plenty of other good advice.

There are ways we can protect our photos and keep them looking good, so we can share our memories with future generations. However, in order to protect your photos, you need to know about the things that will damage your photos so that you can avoid them:

- Water

- Uncontrolled temperatures—normally found in basements and attics

- Sunlight

- High acid levels

- Excessive handling—oil from hands and scratches from being shoved in a drawer somewhere (sound familiar?)

- Magnetic photo albums (you know the kind with the plastic cover page that you peel back, place photos on the sticky surface and replace the plastic)

- Disorganization and lack of labels—making the photos more susceptible to loss and a nightmare for keeping dates in order

Photos of important moments should be protected—how else could you enjoy them 20 years later? So make sure that the only sun and water near your photos are part of your pages.

Your pictures may not live in a castle. Remember however, your photos do need a stable environment so they don't get damaged.

So how do we avoid these demons? Lets go over some of these points.

Water, the Obvious One

No one would store their photos under a sink, right? But what about in a closet on the floor? Is there a bathroom on the other side of the wall that could overflow at any time? Better put your photos up on a shelf. What about under a bed in your bedroom that overlooks a patio and the river beyond? Do you live in a zone prone to flooding? Always keep your photos above floor level and out of the reach of water. Water and photos just don't mix.

Temperatures

Your pictures should live where you do. The attic seems like a neat, romantic place to go to dig through Grandma's memoirs, but actually it's a breeding ground for dust and mold. These are two friends your pictures don't need. Keep your photos in the same temperature-controlled living area where your family lives, ideally organized for all to enjoy!

Photos left in the sunlight will fade and begin to discolor over time. If you look closely at the top of this family picture, you can see how the rest of the photo has faded.

In February 1994, we were living in our little condo in Michigan, while we were building our house. It was a cozy little place and it was a cold winter! However, Lizzy kept us warm with her smile! She loved her cake, so we let her really "get into it"! Because Liz loves to read, she got lots of books for her birthday! We spent a quiet evening, just the family, enjoying her day!

CELEBRATE!

HMM...THIS IS TASTY!

NOW, I'LL ONLY GET A LITTLE...NO ONE WILL SEE...EVEN IF THEY DO...

...IT'S MY BIRTHDAY!!

IT'S YOUR DAY!

Sunlight Can Be Damaging to Your Photos

Sunlight fades photos over time until one day they are gone! On a recent trip to see my parents, I noticed a family picture on my mother's desk. I had seen this picture a million times growing up; it was always a family favorite and a treasured keepsake. I took one look at it and knew the color was different. When I removed it from the frame it had been in for thirty-plus years, I could see a ridge of the original color of the photo at the top. This slight portion had been protected by the frame. The years had already faded the once vibrant photo that held the smiling faces of my family. Decorate your homes with family pictures but only if you have the negative. If you don't, make a color copy of that picture of Grandpa when he was twelve and put the copy in the frame. Protect the original inside a scrapbook. While you're at it, make a copy for other family members that would enjoy it.

Archival Quality Control

You may hear others refer to the importance of being "acid free." This term may seem unclear or confusing. Here's what you need to

Time moves on, children grow up, parents turn grayer, all things change. You can capture the delight of early memories in a scrapbook.

If you aren't organized, you may not have the mementos you need later when making a scrapbook page. If you look closely at this page, you can see an actual sample of Joe's hair from his first haircut.

Joe's First 'Official' Haircut

When Joseph was 5 days old, we brought him home from the hospital and had to cut his sideburns because they were so long! His first official haircut was in May 1985 when he was 7 months old.

know about being acid free and using archival quality products. When photos are processed, they receive a certain amount of acid from the chemicals used for developing. This is normal. You don't want to raise that acid level too high or your pictures will be discolored and ugly. This isn't normal. Buying acid-free products helps you maintain a proper pH level. The tricky part about acid is that it migrates. This means that if you put your photos in safe protector sheets and then put them into a scrapbook that isn't archival quality, you've defeated the purpose and put your pictures at risk. Learning about photo-safe products will enable you to protect your memories for generations to come. (See sidebar later in this chapter for more information regarding photo protection.)

Handling

White cotton gloves make touching your photos really safe since you aren't passing on any fingerprints, which attract dust and other culprits. They also make you look like a professional scrapbooker. Make sure you put them on when viewing your photos in public so everyone will be really impressed, and you will look like you really know what you are doing!

Magnetic Photo Albums

Magnetic photo albums are like thieves, constantly getting a bad rap and deservedly so! They rob your photos of color due to their high-acid content and can destroy them by permanently "gluing" them to the page. Years ago when I learned about the acid-free, archival issue, I had some pictures that I had put in these albums for only a few years. When I removed them (they were already discolored), some of the pictures tore easily and were damaged. Boy, was I happy I had the negatives. Part of the charm of being archivally correct is that it protects your memories without altering them.

Scratches

Scratches mainly occur when photos are carelessly shoved into various places. I'm sorry, but you have to get organized (more about that later). Besides, scratches make your pictures look ugly and unwanted, and this is what we want to avoid!

getting it together

Have you ever gotten involved in a project and discovered you were missing something? I hate when that happens! This is why you have to get organized. (I know, the "O" word again!) Whether it will take an hour, a weekend, or a month, you must not skip this vital process. Here's how to make it easier:

1. **Gather all photos into one spot—** Leave no stone unturned. Check all drawers, boxes, closets and other hiding spots for your pictures. Gather the

memorabilia items also; these should be organized, too. If memorabilia can't be identified, throw it out.

2. **Divide photos into years—**If you have been really negligent, this could be an issue. Look in the pictures for clues as to which month/year it was taken. Remember, the date may have been printed on the back of the photo when it was developed—not when the photo was taken. If you are not sure of the year, narrow it down to the decade.

3. **Divide and conquer—**After each year is grouped, divide them into events: Lexy's first birthday, Joe's first haircut, Cape Cod trip, etc. If you have the occasional photo from when the dog was being cute or the kids did something funny, group those into seasons: Summer '94, Winter '89, etc. If you don't have that many pictures, categorize them chronologically throughout the year. Another choice is to separate them for each child or family member. You could also separate them in categories like vacations, holidays, school days, etc. This will always depend on how many photos you have.

4. **Purchase photo-safe products—** All long-term storage should be acid free and/or archival quality. Photos should not be stored in plastic or vinyl. That plastic container that you swear you will only keep them in for a few short weeks, forget it. I've got your number, and it's something like 5 years before you know it!

5. **Organize memorabilia—**This is your chance to organize all the ticket stubs, programs, and clippings you've saved over the

JILL'S NOTEBOOK

Things to Do

1. Go thru drawers in kitchen and bedrooms for any loose photos.

2. Collect boxes of photos from front hall closet, under beds, and basement.

3. Retrieve box of childhood/college memories from Mom's house.

4. Begin dating the backs of the photos with permanent photo-safe pen.

5. Refer to personal journals for dates and information needed to label photos.

As you can see, the 8½" x 11" is a smaller "canvas" to work with, but this allows ease and convenience in documenting your memories.

years. Letter-size files or envelopes can be used for storage. Also, these can be used for memorabilia that you might want to include. Label these by year to coincide with your other topics.

scrapbook size: the choice is yours

There are two sizes that have become standard in the industry: 8½" x 11" or 12" x 12". Because I own a retail store, I am often asked by customers, "Which one is better?" There are pros and cons to both sizes, with personal preference influencing the final decision.

8½" x 11"

• Most paper is found in this size, but 12" x 12" is catching up fast. However, this size fits in your computer printer, which makes things

Viewing the 12" x 12" page in comparison to the 8½" x 11" above, you can see that in this case a few inches really does make a difference.

An Escape to the Cape

In May 1998, a highly anticipated road trip, took Christine and I to Cape Cod. The weather had been unseasonably cold, but we didn't care. The peace and relaxation that awaited us made up for anything that could have gone wrong.

CAPE COD OR BUST!

You can escape from reality for only so long, but sooner or later, you will have to confront your piles of photos. Arranging them in scrapbooks, along with the stories behind the memories, will make them that much sweeter!

12" x 12"

• The surface area is larger so you can place more photos on the page and have additional room to journal. This usually means having less scrapbooks, which is nice if you are short on storage space.

• There is a range of formats in this size, from three-ring binders to posts or the flex-hinge binding. Choose the one that best fits your style and budget.

• Pattern paper, stickers, and many other embellishments are now being formatted to this larger size, so finding these at your local store is no longer as difficult as it has been in the past.

• This is what I consider a coffee table size. It just seems like it belongs there. Besides, that's where you want it so everyone can enjoy meandering down memory lane.

really easy if you plan to use this technology as a way to record your memories.

• The surface area is smaller and may save you time if you feel the need to fill up the entire page. Although, this philosophy could also work against you for the same reason.

• This size fits on most bookshelves, which makes it handy for storage.

• Scrapbooks come in three standard bindings—the flex hinge strap, 3-ring binder, or post binding. All three types of albums are expandable, which is extremely important when choosing a scrapbook. Top loading sheet protectors are best for versatility and are standard in this size for all of the binding styles mentioned.

Choosing which size is best for you is always a personal preference. I use the larger size (12" x 12") for my family albums. For example, I have albums for vacations, holidays, birthdays, and everyday fun. The standard size (8½" x 11") is the one I use for my children's memoirs, starting with their school years. The

8" x 10" school photos from each grade level can serve as an introduction for the activities of the school year. Also, this size is great for including a certificate or other paper they received, eliminating the need to decorate the rest of the page or have separate storage for these keepsakes. Most items like this come in the standard size anyway!

basic supplies to get you started

An archival quality scrapbook with plenty of PVC-free protector sheets is a must when getting started and should be your first choice.

Your scrapbooks can be as elaborate or as simple as your personality. How you choose to decorate them will be an extension of your individuality and your memories.

Keeping It Safe

To keep your precious memories safe, follow these guidelines.

1. Purchase decorative paper that is acid free. The paper is the basis of your scrapbook and should be acid free, buffered (this helps to reduce acid migration), and lignin-free.

2. Choose a scrapbook with protector sheets that are polypropylene and PVC free.

3. Use acid-free and photo-safe adhesives. Remember that double-sided photo tape or photo corners are the best for photos. No rubber cement or regular tape.

4. Keep your scrapbooks away from damaging conditions, such as water and excessive heat. Always store them in an environment that has a controlled temperature.

5. Label photos (date and place) with a permanent, photo-safe marking pen as soon as possible after being developed.

6. Enjoy, share, and preserve your memories for those you love.

Whatever size you choose, it's important to protect your pages from fingerprints. The point of this is so others can enjoy your photos without ruining them. If they aren't protected and someone has just eaten fried food and reaches for your book, your photos may be ruined. You need to protect your photos from all types of damage.

Adhesives

You should always use some sort of double-sided tape on your pictures. My favorite is pre-cut small squares—place one in each corner of the photo. Dispensers for double-sided tape work great, too. For paper to paper (in the form of embellishments or memorabilia), use an acid-free glue stick. There are many types out there. Just stay away from rubber cement like the plague! Anything that has a foul odor to it most likely contains chemicals that are not safe for your photos.

Cutting Tools

You should have a pair of straight scissors, a personal trimmer (one with a blade you can replace when it becomes dull), and various types of creative-edge scissors. A circle cutter is another great trimmer to have, giving you perfect circles every time!

Archival Pens

"Archival pens" means that they are permanent, waterproof, fade-proof, and light fast. Having a bunch of different colors and tips is always handy. There are many different types on the market; some are very addicting so you should proceed with caution.

cropping photos

Cropping photos can be a great way to enhance a picture, if done properly. Remember the idea is to make the photo look better. Here are a few guidelines:

REASONS TO CROP
1. To remove dark shadows, distracting images, or undesirable scenery that is detracting from subject.
2. To trim any excess or unneccessary background footage.
3. To bring a photo into balance with its subject.
4. To accentuate the focal point in the picture.
WHEN IN DOUBT, DON'T CUT IT OUT!

Because each photograph was staged the same way, this page looks good with all the photos cut into silhouettes. Generally speaking, there should be some variety to the shapes on each scrapbook page, for best visual interest.

- Never, ever, crop a Polaroid. This may seem obvious, but you never can be sure. If a polaroid is cut, the chemicals leak out and ruin your now ex-photo.

- Never crop a picture you don't have the negative for, especially old photos.

- If there is dead space in the picture that wouldn't be missed, such as too much grass or sky, go ahead and crop a little, being careful to keep the subject in balance.

- Don't crop a photo that would alter the historical value of the picture. Backgrounds add to the story. You may want to see that old '76 Pinto you had in college later on. However, if you have a million photos with that old car in the background and one might benefit from being cropped, go ahead and crop it.

- If cropping would help create balance for the subject, then go ahead and trim. You can fix many pictures this way. Be careful not to get too close to the subject. Leave even amounts of space on all sides of the photo outside the subject, if possible.

- Cropping a picture may enable you to remove something distracting from the background. Use the previous guidelines I have mentioned as they apply.

silhouetting and shaping photos

I love to occasionally silhouette pictures, but be careful not to overdo it. As I said, this may improve the picture by completely removing something that is distracting or boring in the background. Here are the secrets to this:

- Scissors with short blades work best when silhouetting. They provide more control and precision when trimming delicate images.

GUIDELINES FOR MATTING PHOTOS

1. A photo has enough images going in it that it doesn't need an uneven edge (border) to throw off the flow of the picture.
2. Trimming photographs with creative-edge scissors can be very distracting to the images in your photograph.
3. Creative-edge scissors should be used for frames, borders, and other embellishments.

• Not every nook and cranny needs to be traced. Don't trim into tiny areas, leave them as a whole instead.

• Do not cut into the image. Instead, leave a slight rim of the background, just enough so your eye has the chance to see the edge of the image. This is more visually pleasing, unless you are using this technique as a form of weight loss in your pictures, then go ahead and trim off a little extra hip and thigh!

• Proceed with caution when shaping pictures with templates. Basic shapes like ovals and circles are great, but most photos aren't enhanced with con-

fusing shapes. Keep it simple and make sure the body of the shape is large enough to enclose the entire focal point of the photo. Remember, when in doubt, don't cut it out!

• Choose shapes that have something to do with the theme. Look inside your photo for ideas of shapes that can be repeated.

• There aren't too many things I find more distracting in photos than trimming the image with patterned scissors. Don't get me wrong, I love these products. I own most of what's good on the market today. Look closely at the difference in the samples on this page. You can clearly see how much better and how much easier you focus on the subject in the photo when the edges are kept straight.

becoming unequal

John F. Kennedy once said, "Every man is created equal, with an equal opportunity to become unequal." With the knowledge you are gaining through this book, this is your chance to become unequal. To rise above the norm, look within your soul, remember the past, and document for the future. History has always allowed us to learn from others' mistakes, revel in others' glories, and share in the common bond we have as human beings in search of happiness. Scrapbooking can be a written expression of our life's journey.

embarking on a splendid journey

The most important part of what you will add to your scrapbook is the who, what, where, when, and why of your photos. That means if you are in the other room, at the grocery store, or no longer available, whoever is looking at your scrapbook will be able to tell what was happening in the pictures. Where were you? When was this? Who were all the people in the pictures? And any other funny tidbits you may want to pass on. With the many unique ways we have to decorate our scrapbook pages, we must never lose sight of this one fact: our pictures must remain the focus of our books. Although we have the chance to display our personalities through the pages of our scrapbooks for our posterity to see, they will never truly know us if we do not record the details of our lives and beckon them to look into our faces and see the individuality that lies within our pictures. Begin now by embarking on this splendid journey of scrapbooking and leave your family and loved ones something they will treasure through all time—their recorded memories.

How we define ourselves is evidenced in the way we record our memories. The way we journal and the way we decorate our pages are both telling manifestations of our personality.

A Splendid Journey

After leaving Cape Cod, eventually bound for home, we began our journey with no particular place in mind. We spent time in: Newport, Rhode Island Mystic and Stonington, Connecticut parts of New Jersey the scenic route through New York in the Catskill Mountains

(above) overlooking the water in Mystic, Connecticut (right) Christine and I with Mystic behind us, on our way to Stonington for lunch and shopping

(top left) in front of Gardenworks in Mystic, CT (bottom left) the Water Street Market and FUN, a great place to shop for cool stuff (above) Diane Marsh, who we named "the pie goddess" because she made the most incredible banana creme pie we have ever tasted

Frequently Asked Questions

Q. WHAT KIND OF GLUE SHOULD I USE ON MY PHOTOS?

A. Actually, it's best not to use glue with your photos, but rather you should use double-sided tape. Acid-free glue can be used on your paper embellishments in your scrapbook.

Q. CAN I PUT NEWSPAPER CLIPPINGS IN MY SCRAPBOOK?

A. Newspaper is printed on paper that has a very high acid content. That is one of the reasons it deteriorates so quickly. I recommend having it copied onto acid-free paper. It can also be color copied to retain the authentic "yellowed" appearance that is frequently desired.

Q. I BOUGHT A SCRAPBOOK YEARS AGO THAT DOES NOT HAVE PROTECTIVE SHEETS. IS IT SAFE TO USE?

A. That depends on whether or not it is made of archival quality products. If not, then it is best to invest in a newer book that will protect your photos over time—otherwise you may ruin your photos. If it is made of archival quality products, then you might contact the company that made it to see if they have since made protective sheets for it. I would always recommend having a scrapbook with protective sheets.

Q. HOW CAN I UTILIZE MY COMPUTER IN SCRAPBOOKING?

A. The two most popular ways to use a computer for this art is to either use it for journaling (whether it is printed directly on the paper you will mount photos on or to cut and paste) or to use clip art programs that will allow you to make frames or other decorations.

Q. WHAT TYPE OF PEN SHOULD I USE TO LABEL THE BACKS OF MY PHOTOS?

A. Never use a ball point pen or pencil on your photos. A photo marking pen that is permanent and made to write directly on photographic paper is best.

Q. DO ALL MY PAGES HAVE TO BE DECORATED?

A. Your scrapbook should reflect your personal style. Choose simple designs and colors to compliment your photos and enhance the essence of your personality.

Principles of Design

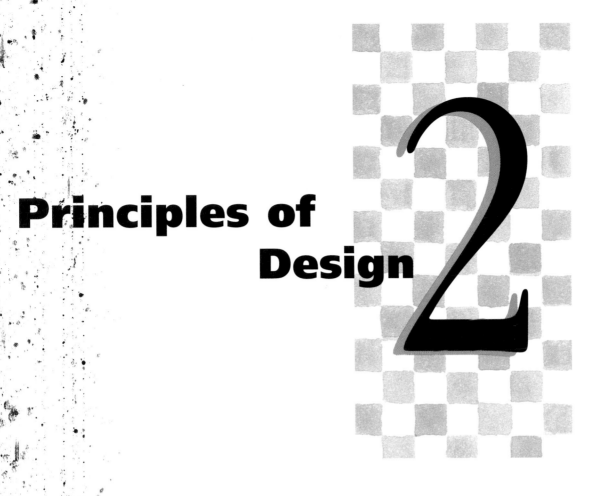

THE KEY TO ANY GOOD RELATIONSHIP IS understanding. As you embark on developing a relationship with scrapbook art, it's best to fully understand what it is that you are doing. Once this realization takes place, ideas start to flow and come more easily. With this chapter, you will learn the elements of design layout and begin to understand the relationship this art has to your life. In reference to the quote we've all heard, I am not just going to give you a fish (an idea), I am going to teach you to fish. And once you have mastered the technique, you will never be hungry for ideas again!

make it memorable

Why is it that some scrapbook page layouts look better than others? Sometimes we can stare at a page and just know that it isn't quite right, but we're not sure why. Does it seem too crowded? Or even too bare? Is your eye being drawn away from the focus to one distracting thing? If you are having to obsess over your page for any length of time, then something isn't right.

The key to attractive pages (ones that look right) is organization and eye appeal. We all know what this is like, and we've seen this in other aspects of our lives. Think of those times when you've

seen someone on the street who's overdressed and you've thought (go ahead, admit it), "Where's the clothes police when you need them?" You know the kind of people that I mean, overaccessorized and a big ol' mess! If they would just take off that extra necklace or remove the frilly hat, then maybe the psychedelic suit with the belt and the extra lace collar wouldn't be quite so distracting. Less is definitely more!

This chapter will teach you how to give your layouts the focus they need. This doesn't mean that you need to go back and change everything you've already done. Just live and learn and move on down the road to better layouts. If you are just beginning, this will allow you to get off to a fabulous start. You are finally getting the horse before the cart!

The theme of these pages was chosen because our son was born the night the Detroit Tigers won the American League Pennant. My husband *always* brings this up—it's the focus of this memory for him (my focus was pain).

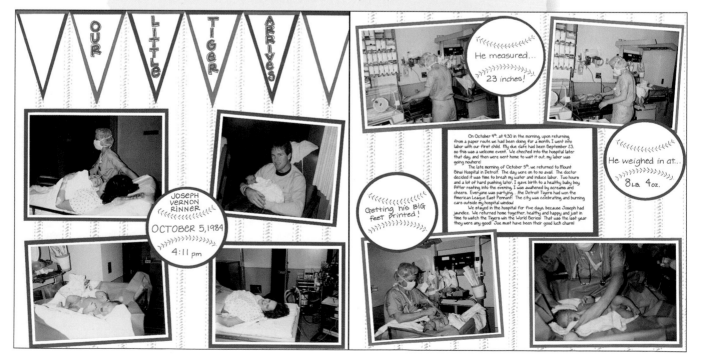

Begin by opening your eyes and your heart to the feelings that your favorite memories generate.

creating the focus

The key to meaningful pages begins with choosing a focus. Giving your layout a focus is the key to making everything else come together. With the focus in mind, the memory flows easier and the layout becomes a living history. To determine the focus, ask yourself these questions:

• What do I want to emphasize with this memory—the feeling or the theme?

• How many pages will my layout be— one or two, or more?

• Why did I take these pictures? What was my intention?

• Is there anything special about this memory that stands out in my mind?

Take, for example, pictures from a baby's birth. This is usually an incredible activity to be a part of. Was there an emergency situation involved? Were you giving birth on the side of the road? Or was everything just as you had planned—love and joy and relief all at once? The focus of your page layout can bring any of these feelings alive.

The night my son was born has always given my husband a story to tell. We were living in the Detroit area at the time and were Tiger fans—and they were on a winning streak. It was October 1984, and it was late in the afternoon when he was finally delivered. I was thrilled and relieved after 34 hours of labor. As the evening wore on, I was awakened by cheering nurses and a city gone mad! Were they celebrating the birth of our son also? No! The Detroit Tigers had won the American League Pennant and were heading to the World Series, which they went on to win that year.

Whenever the story of the birth of our son comes up, this is the main thing we talk about. This is his claim to fame. Do you see what I'm getting at? Here is the theme for the perfect layout. It helps tell the story and bring it to life! This is the focus of that memory. Once it was chosen, decisions such as color, title, and embellishments were easy to choose. The focus for your page gives direction to all your other choices.

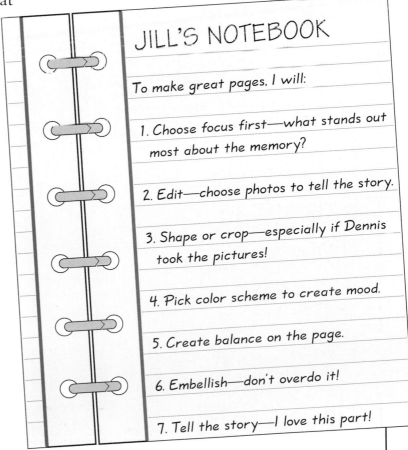

JILL'S NOTEBOOK

To make great pages, I will:

1. Choose focus first—what stands out most about the memory?

2. Edit—choose photos to tell the story.

3. Shape or crop—especially if Dennis took the pictures!

4. Pick color scheme to create mood.

5. Create balance on the page.

6. Embellish—don't overdo it!

7. Tell the story—I love this part!

These 6 pages are a good example of a complete layout. 1) The first page is the title page for "Lizzy's Art Party." It establishes what the memory was about. It has a sample of the invitation and features the birthday girl and her cake. Also, this page establishes the color scheme and the focus for the layout. 2) Here the chronological story begins. This is the first activity of the party. 3) These are the guests that attended. 4) This page details of different activities of the party and gives information about them. Also, the page is decorated in the same theme of the craft that was made during the party. 5) Here we had our cake and ate it too. 6) Finally, the presents were opened and the treats were handed out as the guests left.

organize and edit your photos

Obviously, every picture you take in your lifetime will not end up in a scrapbook. Some pictures are not even focused and are easy to discard. But how do you decide which pictures should make the cut and which ones should be left out?

First, gather pictures from an event, such as a birthday party. Then separate the photos into mini subjects within the event: pictures of the table and cake before the party started, the guests, games being played, candle blowing and cake eating, presents being opened, guests leaving, the aftermath, and finally, the cleanup. Keep the pictures as chronological as possible. This is where organization comes in. The reader should be able to determine how the event was played out. Remember, you are giving an historical account of your life.

If the layout will be more than two pages, certain photographs can be chosen for a title page. These should be the pictures that give a glimpse into the story that is to follow. Think of it as the "introduction." All the pertinent historical information can be on this page (the when and where). Details will follow on subsequent pages.

Next, go back and choose the pictures that best represent what

was going on. Things to consider: clear images, good color, accurate representation of the event, visibility of the subject, value to the story, expressions of people in the photo. Remember, not every picture you've taken is worthy of a place in your scrapbook. Choose those that will help tell the story of your life.

In a perfect world, we would have great pictures of it all, but life is not always perfect. If all the pictures are awful or you don't have enough to even put a page together, don't despair. Life's memories are not only about photos. There is probably a lot you can tell about the event without ever showing a picture. And remember that a bad picture is better than no picture at all.

If you are in need of more photos from an event, consider adding pictures that can be taken after the fact. If you forgot to take pictures from the first day of school, you can go back and photo-

Choosing a variety of shapes for your photos gives your layout the diversity it needs to be as exciting as a ride down the Alpine Slide!

On Dennis' 40th birthday, September 1st 1997, he wanted to do something thrilling. So, we took him to Park City for a swervy trip down the Alpine slide. It wasn't very death defying but the views on top of the mountain were beautiful!

What goes up . . .

. . . must come down!

ALPINE SLIDE

Not every photo needs to be cropped. Refer back to the focus you have chosen to determine if shaping would be acceptable or not.

have a mix of sizes and shapes on the page.

When deciding to shape the photo, whether it will be a silhouette line or a shape traced from a template, keep in mind your layout focus. Would shaping the photo coincide with the theme? For example, a sports theme that involved a round ball, such as basketball or soccer, would be a perfect place to find circle-shaped photos. And remember, only use your creative-edge scissors to trim your borders and embellishments—not your photographs. The random edge they create is much too distracting to the image of your photograph.

graph the school, the teacher, the kids in the classroom together—and when doing the layout, add the story from the first day of school to preserve that memory.

cropping and shaping

Once you have determined which photos are appropriate for your layout, you can begin cropping or shaping them. Not all photos need to be cropped; only crop to enhance the picture itself. Refer back to the focus you have chosen to determine if shaping would be acceptable or not.

Be sure that cropping the picture will enhance it and not detract from it. Sometimes merely rounding a corner will give the picture enough softness and improvement. The most eye appealing layouts

choosing the color scheme

As with the shaping of photographs, the color you add to your layout should enhance the photos and make them look better. Color plays a big part in determining where your eye is drawn first. It can also make certain objects in your photo seem more obvious. This strategy could work against you, if it is something you don't want to focus on.

Certain holidays are associated with specific colors, but this does not mean that those popular colors for the holiday would look the best with your pictures. Red and green may be standard Christmas colors, but if you decorate your house and tree with a different color scheme, then red and green would not be the best choice. Using the colors that match and enhance the pictures and adding titles that pull everything together will help keep the focus in your layout.

In this example, "A Mooey Christmas," the colors black, white, and red are more suitable to the cow theme than the traditional Christmas colors.

Always keep your color choices simple, choosing a dominant color with two or three secondary colors. Place your photos on top of the colors you've chosen and make sure that your eye is being drawn to what it is you want to focus on. Once again the colors chosen should support, not dominate, the theme or feeling of your layout.

sign. They are the sign of correct weight and balance. Think of these scales and how the weight needs to be evenly distributed so that the scales don't topple over. Your page layout works the same way.

If the page was cut into equal sections, whether it be in halves, thirds, or quarters, each section should have the same "weight." The arrangement could be a mirror image of each section, or it could be a random grouping. Either way, your eye should be able to flow through the layout without being drawn to one side because it's too heavy.

Each item that you place on your page has a visual weight also. Each photograph, journaling segment, or other embellishment adds weight. Keep the scales in mind, and aim to keep each section of your page balanced. If a page is too top heavy, it will appear off balance, ready to tip. It is better to have more weight on the bottom of the page to stabilize it, but

layout and balance

Understanding balance is one of the most important elements for creating a great layout each time, and it is easy to learn. Since I am a Libra, I often think of the scales associated with this astrological

Don't have a cow—you don't have to decorate your Christmas pages in red and green! This "mooey" cool pattern was added to the borders and lettering to accentuate the cow print theme.

This page illustrates how important balance is—you don't want to make your page layout seem like it will come tumbling down. You can see how the layout for this page has been separated into thirds to balance the visual weight.

remember that equal balance should be your goal.

When positioning items on your page, keep in mind the theme that you are focusing on. Fun, whimsical themes may allow you to have a little more freedom in your placement. Placing photos at an angle can be much more pleasing to the eye than lining them up straight, but never angle the pictures too much, where it becomes hard to focus on the images. Keep in mind that if you have to tilt your head to study the detail in the picture, it's angled too much. My rule of thumb for life is "less is more." Don't create a layout that will overpower the focus of your pictures.

Pulling It off the Page

"Pulling" photos or other elements of the layout off the page

This page is a good example of "pulling" your photos off the page. It's also a good use of space, allowing you to fit many full-sized photos to fit on one page.

The five pictures and the guest list have been used to create this sectioned collage. Notice how the balloon punch visually extends the balloon centerpiece that was cut off when the picture was taken.

not only gives you more room to include additional photos and allows for more space that can be used for journaling but it also creates interest for the eye by drawing it out to the edge of the page and invites your eye to wander. This technique works best if the story continues onto another page.

Collages

Placing items edge-to-edge to create a collage enables you to fit a great deal of information and many photos into a condensed space. This format works best if all the pictures are from one specific theme and can flow together in the storytelling. Items can also be separated by slight borders. Remember to reserve at least one spot within the layout to identify the items on the page.

Some colors and patterns add more visual power than others, such as the checkerboard frames shown here. Take things like this into account when creating visual balance in your layout.

Scrapbooking, Craft or Art?

Depending upon your point of view, scrapbooking your memories could be either a craft or an art. Making the distinction between the two is key. As a craft, scrapbooking is a hobby, but it can still seem like a chore at times—no extra words or thoughts, limited color schemes and commercialized embellishments. It seems to lack that added flair. But as an art, it's a love. There are details added, passion expressed, insight revealed and soul baring represented. There is quality first, then quantity. Variety and pattern are in abundance and the reader is drawn into the life of the artist. Once again, the memory becomes real. The choice is yours. Will you be a crafter or an artist?

Overlapping

Overlapping connects the images together and creates an easy path for the eye to follow. This type of photo placement is a good way to link items that you want to appear related within the layout, such as a chronological sequence.

Symmetrical Placement

Symmetrical designs are when one half of the layout is identical or similar in shape and weight to the opposite side of the layout. This type of placement keeps the eye flowing back and forth.

Scattered Designs

Mixing items on the page, whether they are placed straight or on an angle, creates some of the most interesting designs for layouts. Just make sure that your visual weight is balanced. If you must tilt your head to view it, then straighten it out a little.

There are many different ways to design a scrapbook page. Let your focus be your guide when deciding how your page elements will be placed. The format of a page will lend a certain mood also, just as color does, so consider the chosen theme.

Follow the instincts that you use in other aspects of your life. I like to compare decorating a page to how I would decorate a room. All the furniture would not be placed on one side of the room, there would be a comfortable flow of objects. Observe layout and balance around you and allow it to inspire you to create great scrapbook pages!

embellishments

Adding embellishments to your pages in the form of stickers, die cuts, pattern paper, or

An "ing"-credible trip... picnicing napping antiquing talking watching discovering exploring dining listening meditating adventuring expressing feeling receiving energizing dreaming believing... and just being!

"Tomorrow's life is too late... live today."
—Martial

Cape Cod Bay
MAY 1998

This double page layout includes a collage of pictures on the right and a symmetrical design, with various shapes, to the left. Variety in placement is the key to "ing"-credible pages!

punch art can enhance the look of your page or detract from it. Think of it like decorating a small room. How many mixed styles of furniture can you place in it before it starts to look overdone? The elements would begin to clash, and confusion would ensue. Remember that our rule for life "less is more," definitely applies here.

Adding embellishments to your page is like accessorizing a living space. Every room needs a focal point and so does every layout. Ask yourself, do I want to notice the sticker art first, or is the memory more important? You usually know the answer to this question right away. Choose your accessories carefully and don't mix too many styles. No more than two categories of accessories is a good

rule of thumb (categories being identified as pattern paper, stickers, die cut art, memorabilia, etc.). If you use stickers and pattern paper on one page, adding a die cut may be too confusing for one layout.

Embellishments can flow and change from page to page, just as they do in separate rooms in a home, just limit the style of them on each layout for the most pleasing look. Never forget that your pictures should always remain the focus and embellishments should merely enhance the storytelling—not take over. The personality of a page hinges on its words and embellishments. When adding these two aspects to your page, ask yourself, "Is it saying exactly what I want, both visually and verbally?"

We went to all the action-adventure shows and saw how all the stunts are done in the movies. Everything looks so realistic!

AT THE INDIANA JONES STUNT SHOW

LIGHTS... CAMERA... ACTION... FIRE!

WITH NO WARNING, WE WERE TRAPPED IN A FLASH FLOOD... MOVIE STYLE!

The addition of the die cuts as embellishments are not only part of the journaling surface but mimic the theme inside of each picture.

7 Steps to a Perfect Layout

Here's a quick review of the thought process behind designing a perfect layout every time.

1. Choose focus
2. Edit pictures
3. Shape and crop
4. Choose color scheme
5. Create layout and balance
6. Embellish
7. Journal

finishing a page

After the page has been assembled and space has been allotted for journaling, it is now time to tell the story. To decide what information should be included in your story ask yourself some basic questions: When was this? Who are the people in the pictures? Where were they, and what were they doing? Did anything interesting happen that stands out in your memory and makes the story come alive again? The answers to these questions will bring this treasured memory to life. Add meaningful quotes, use song titles or catchy phrases, and, most importantly, add the words that will draw the reader into your life. The written word lends power and thought to the moment. This is the gift we will leave behind when we are gone, the gift of history.

do what you love

If all these guidelines are making you crazy, throw them aside and do what you love. Principles of design are great if they can help us create a space that makes us more comfortable with who we are. The moment that you are not pleased with what you are doing is the time to reevaluate the circumstances and do what comes naturally. These principles are meant to help you define your scrapbooking personality.

A scrapbook is essentially your life story. How will it read when you're gone? Exciting? Full of passion for life? Adventurous? Elegant? Chatty? Funky? Make sure it's a reflection of you.

Remember that normally life isn't always sunshine and roses. Sometimes we

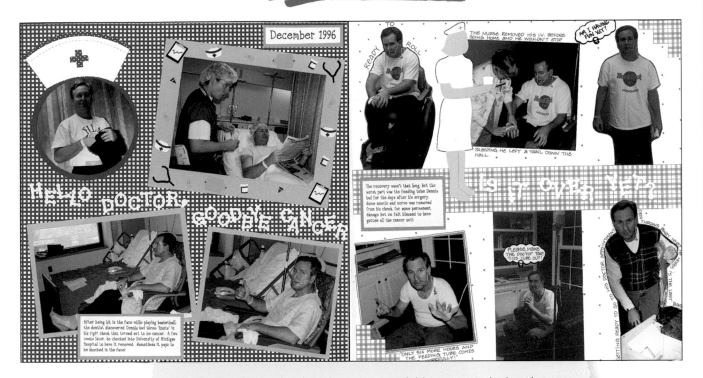

Scrapbooking the hard times we'd like to put behind us is just as important us documenting our exciting moments we want to remember. Reviewing these types of pages in a scrapbook reminds us of the challenges we have overcome and gained experience from.

have to battle difficult times, but it's usually through these trials that we become the people of character that will be our legacy. You should also scrapbook those hard times, documenting the challenges that were met face-to-face and conquered. Our scrapbook will become a true historical account of our life's joys and challenges. We will leave a personal history that will be meaningful to future generations—and treasured for years to come.

Each time I have the opportunity to visit an antique shop on my quest for

hidden treasures, I'm saddened when I see old photographs of families that are discarded and lost. Unfortunately, the people in these photos usually aren't identified and their stories remain untold. Also, I'm intrigued by the possibility of the life that they might have lived. It often makes me wonder if there are pictures out there of my ancestors, those who have gone before and created their own legacy. These photographs should be immortalized within a scrapbook designed to share that family history.

Frequently Asked Questions

Q. WHAT RULES ARE THE MOST IMPORTANT ONES TO FOLLOW?

A. The rules of purchasing archival products are the most important ones to follow to protect your pictures. Otherwise, there are only principles to guide you—not limit you. Let your memories create the mood, allowing creativity and self expression be the main rules you follow.

Q. SHOULD EACH BACKGROUND COLOR OR PATTERN BE THE SAME THROUGHOUT THE LAYOUT?

A. No! Variety is the spice of life. Whenever you have two pages that will be viewed together as a double-page spread, they can match if the subject is the same. If the mood of the pictures has changed, feel free to make them different.

Q. CAN I USE STICKERS TO DECORATE MY PAGES?

A. The embellishments that you use should always be secondary to the pictures that are the true focus of your scrapbook. Eliminate the need to over decorate the pages.

Q. SHOULD I PUT BLURRY PHOTOS IN MY SCRAPBOOK?

A. It would be ideal to have the best photos in your scrapbook, but sometimes a photo that is out of focus is better than not having the memory documented. Choose the photos that best represent the memory you are sharing.

Q. MUST I LABEL EVERY PICTURE ON EVERY PAGE WITH WHO IS IN THEM?

A. If you have a page where there are four pictures and the same people are in each picture, then you only need to identify those in the photos once. If the people are different, then identify each person by name. Do not list yourself as "me" all the time, because in the future someone may not know who "me" was.

Q. SHOULD THE COLORS I CHOOSE FOR MY PAGE MATCH THE COLORS IN MY PHOTOS?

A. Generally speaking no, because one color can become too dominant. Balance color and let the subject of the photo be your guide.

Photo Journaling

WE'VE ALL KNOWN GREAT STORYTELLERS.
And we've all listened in awe as they have rattled off, from memory, story after interesting story of their lives and the lives of others. Why is it that some people just have the knack for remembering and telling stories? I can barely remember what I did last week, let alone relay the information to someone else at a later date.

In this chapter, I will share with you some creative ways to begin telling the story found in each picture you possess. Words make these memories come alive. Without them, they can end up as meaningless images of a life passed.

telling the story

One story I remember is when a woman came into my scrapbook store seeking advice on how to begin the scrapbook adventure. She had brought her accumulation of photographs with her. Everything was perfectly placed in beautiful albums, organized and pretty. There were pictures of children, laughing and playing, and pictures of a family skiing together. Were they in Switzerland? Aspen? Or at some local ski resort? Either way, I couldn't tell. There wasn't a word or a date to be found.

So I inquired, "Where was this? Who are these people? What are they doing? Why are they laughing?" Of course, she was sitting in front of me and could answer all of my questions. But what happens if she's not around? How would I ever know the answers to the questions I had? What if she went out to run errands? How would I ever know the story within her engaging pictures?

Including journaling on your page is not just a whim—it is an essential part of retelling the story. Give the pertinent information necessary to inform the reader about the memory.

- When did the memory take place?
- What was happening?
- Is there a story to tell?

Pictures alone do not give all this type of information—you must include the details.

Many people have commented to me that they feel their stories aren't interesting enough to talk about. I used to think that same thing. One day I was listening to my brother recount a story he had told his Sunday School class. He told it with such exuberance that it sounded exciting, even though it was pretty standard life stuff. I commented on how I didn't have any stories to tell, and asked why he had so many great ones, when we grew up in the same family? His answer changed my view. He said that everyone has a story to tell, and he proceeded to ask me questions, drawing out story after story in my mind. I was hooked!

Not only does everyone have a story to tell, but so does every picture. Look at your pictures and ask yourself: What was happening? When was this taken? Who are the people in the photographs? How old are they? Where were the pictures taken? Why were these pictures taken? Was it a special occasion? Did something funny or unusual happen that day? What was the general feeling of the event? All the answers can help you tell the story of your pictures . . . the story of your wonderful life. Remember to stick to the point of each individual layout and don't ramble on with unnecessary information that no one would need to know. Keep all your comments flattering to those in the photos. Otherwise, the only one who looks bad is the storyteller!

Here are some creative ways to help you become not only the scrapbooker but the storyteller in your family!

Start with the Who, When, and Where of Your Pictures

This seems basic, but we all look at our pictures and think "I'll never forget this moment." Ha! Unless you have nothing else filling up your brain, you are bound to forget. Write notes to yourself as soon as your pictures are developed. Not every layout needs to have a long story with it. Sometimes just answering these few questions (who? when? where?) recounts enough of the event. While traveling, keep a travel journal with you to record all the information that you otherwise will forget the second you get home.

"I Scream, You Scream, We All Scream for Ice Cream" works great for the theme of this page. You can use popular phrases that best illustrate the mood and feeling of your layout.

I... YOU... we all... **Scream** ...FOR ICE CREAM!

BEN & JERRY'S · CAPE COD, MASS.

A trip to Cape Cod wouldn't be complete without a trip to Ben & Jerry's Ice cream shop. Yum! We also had great ice cream at Herbie's in Provincetown. Christine and I had the best time!

This page shows all of the activities that make up our favorite vacation each year. When making a page like this, the pictures can be taken ahead of time with the theme in mind, planning ahead to get photos from each activity, or as an afterthought, compile the pictures that tell as much of the story as possible.

Make a "Things To Do List" or a "What We Like To Do" Page

These types of lists can be made for everyday life or a special activity or trip that takes place each year as a tradition. If you don't have photos from each item on the "list," tell a little bit of the memory and add a sticker in a matching theme to add something visual to the page.

Conduct an Interview with Someone Who Was There

Interview people of all ages and let them share their favorite part about the event. Everyone has a different point of view, especially children, and their words may be able to shed some light on the activity. Ask for just one adjective to describe the event as a form of simple journaling on your page. A Dictaphone works great for this task and the tape will become a memory itself. My friend Scarlett did this just last year before her grandma died, and she now treasures the recording of her grandma's voice saying, "Bye-bye, I'm going home now."

Do the People in the Pictures Appear To Be Saying Something?

If your photos could talk what would they say? Realistic or not, this is a great way to personalize photographs for your

Hangin' with Friends

We spent the weekend with the Tenney's. The men watched sports, the kids played Nintendo and Kelley and I had fun hanging out, as we always do. We spent a good portion of the night before Dennis' birthday glued in front of the TV watching the world respond to the shocking news that Princess Diana was killed in a car accident in Paris.

Trent and Dennis

J.J. and Lizzy had a great time together! Joe kept Matt and David busy wrestling and playing video games, while Lexy and Brooke hung out together in the "second generation girlfriend" style!

Not every page in your scrapbook needs to be from an exciting event. Sometimes you may just want to highlight and remember moments spent in the company of good friends.

scrapbook. Your pictures will speak to you and give you clues as to what actually may have been said or something witty that can be added for entertainment! Animals are great fun to add dialogue to.

Song Titles Make Great Page Titles

From pop to rock, jazz to oldies, and children's tunes, song titles can make any page come to life. They can be songs that were playing at the time of the event ("They're playing our song!") or any others that merely fit the memory. Lyrics that are apropos to the event can make the memory more real.

Phrasal Congestion?

Use a coined phrase or word that reminds you of the event. Sometimes the word of the moment is a great way to capture trends of the time. Word plays, silly phrases, or private jokes can be hilarious to read later on. Usually these things are forgotten quickly. Write your notes in a travel journal, daily planner, or wallet, so they will not be misplaced. If your words and ideas have been written down, your pictures can speak to you and give you clues as to what may have been said or even something witty that can be added for entertainment! If your photos could talk, what would they say?

Take Pictures of Your Surroundings for Documentation and History

I love to take pictures of my perennial garden each season, not only to capture it in bloom but to look at in the winter time and daydream about spring. Take pictures inside your home, not only for a great historical layout page, but for a fresh eye on how to redecorate a room. Also, photograph special heirloom items that you treasure. Not everyone in your family had the pleasure of having your grandma's china or your great aunt's needlepoint. Take pictures of each family treasure and create a layout page complete with photos of the item and the ancestor they came from. Afterwards, make color copies for other family members.

JILL'S NOTEBOOK

car trip to Cape Cod
somewhere approaching Albany. NY
Conversation at 1:39 pm (having been on the road since 4 am)

—Joe is starving
—Lizzy is crying because her seatbelt is hurting her
—Lexy is crying because the window is open and she can't sleep
—Ian wants to know if we're there yet (we aren't)
—Grandma is trying to listen to Rush
—Jill is driving (sanity questionable)

**travel journals are great places to capture quotes that really reveal the essence of the trip!

Include Invitations, Cards and Letters to Bring a Personal Side to the Story

Birthdays are a great time to save the cards received, but other moments in our lives can be remembered this way also. Get well or sympathy cards can bring back the feelings of support felt in our time of need. Letters written while away from our loved ones are an excellent source of the chronological information of our lives. Save letters of friendship, love, appreciation, or notes written home from camp. These can be mounted on a page to create their own layout or tucked inside a pocket page.

Use Poetry and Quotes to Capture the Feeling of the Event

Poetry, whether personal or famous, can bring a certain feeling to any layout. If you are poetic, write a poem about a specific event, or enlist the help of someone else who was involved. Quotes are also an excellent way to enhance the feeling of any memory.

Popular Phrases Can Catch Your Attention

Appropriate slang words of the moment can add personality to page titles ("Like, totally. . .!") and so can popular phrases. Titles such as "A Star Is Born," "Way to Go," or "Boys Will Be Boys" can spark interest in any layout.

Save Newspapers from Day of an Event and Recreate the Headline

Your personal family history can be intertwined with the headlines of

Actually, there's nothing scarier than letting your memories be forgotten over time. Photo journaling captures the details of the memories that make up the history of our lives. Pictures of snow? You'd think it was February! But the chosen colors and title phrase let you know it was anything but expected!

the moment. Recreate the headline in a page layout format and add your own family history, replacing famous figures in the news with those in your life.

Hindsight Is 20/20

Now that the event has passed, your perspective of it is probably much different than when it took place. This knowledge can help you share the lesson that was encountered during this event. Add this new perspective to your photo journaling so you can realize the difference this event made in your life. However, it is important to journal what the moment was like in your pictures, not just your opinion of the event years later.

Create Travel Pages

For travel pages, document on the page what day it was. For example, day one, day two and so forth can be added to the corner of a page in a small box to show the sequence of events that took place.

Save Programs and Ticket Stubs

Plays, concerts, and sporting events are loads of fun and times we want to remember. If pictures were not taken at the event, save the program and ticket stubs (test them with a pH testing pen first) and add them to your page layout; be sure to include a journaling segment of what transpired.

Top Ten Reasons Why... We Love San Diego Zoo

10. Where else can you go to be in Hog Heaven?

9. You can observe sea lions being more obedient than kids.

8. You can ride a bus to save your feet.

7. You get to see a mouse house made of bread (& get the recipe).

6. You can see someone who looks fatter in a bathing suit than you.

Tara · Michael · Christine · Lexy

5. You get to take your picture with a distant relative.

Ali · Joe · Lexy

3. You can pet animals and get slobbered on at the petting zoo!

Lizzy · Christine

4. You get to ride in a stroller even if you're not a baby.

1. You'll be stunned at how many animals there are!

2. You get to see how you'd look as a bear.

Make the memory come alive but don't forget to:

1. Add humorous quotes that expand the details of the day.

2. Make note of the people in the pictures.

3. If a person is in more than one picture on a page, it's not necessary to label him or her each time if it is obvious that it's the same person.

4. Add comments that coincide with facial expressions in the photo.

Let Children Add Their Two Cents

Art work, interviews, commentary or explanations from children can add insight as well as humor to any situation. It is very important to record their comments verbatim, rather than adding our interpretation of what they said. If they are young and still have not mastered the fine skills of speech, place in parenthesis next to the real the way they pronounced it. For example, when my son, Joe, was little he didn't say his L's correctly, so when he said "luggage," he pronounced it "yuggage."

Steal David Letterman's Idea and Create a Top Ten List

He does it, why can't you? Create a top ten list of anything you want. Plan and take the pictures to match your list or reverse the process and make your list from photos you already have from any event.

Write a Letter to Yourself or Someone Else

Document your feelings or those of any family member (especially a child) in a time of joy or sorrow. This may help them get through a trying time later on when they recall the challenge that was faced. Remember that not only happy times should be documented in your scrapbook. This is your life and everyone has challenges.

Check Brochures from Gift Shops for Historical Information

Not only will you find pictures that you may not have taken of the points of interest, but there is always interesting information that may help you add to the feeling of the event. Historical facts, statistics, or details may be added to give information about the place you visited. Add quotes to give added emotion to what it was like or what you may have learned when you first made the memory.

Movie Titles Make Great Page Titles

Hollywood has produced millions of movies in the past that may or may not have entertained us but can certainly provide ideas for a title page. Check the back of your local television guide where all the movies are listed for ideas.

Create Before/After Pages

Take pictures before and after any event, such as a haircut, dental work, a makeover, parties, redecorating, a garden, dress up for Hal-

loween or play, growth spurts in animals or children (place them standing next to the same inanimate object in each picture so the difference will be noticed), a sports game played (clean and dirty contrast), or any other activity where this would be appropriate.

Create Then/Now Pages To Bridge the Gap in Time

This is especially effective when a great length of time has passed between the two pictures. Take pictures of old friends, pets, houses you have lived in, places you have visited/revisited, places of work or sentimental value.

Make a Timeline

Create a timeline of a day, a month, a year or a lifetime. This is a nice way to get a lifetime in a small album where one pic-

Sometimes "it takes two" hours to think of a great title for a page. Cut that time to two minutes with the help of song or movie titles easily found in your home. Check the T.V. guide or CDs for titles that make great pages.

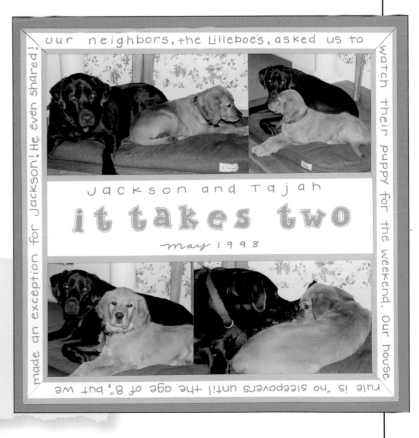

our neighbors, the Lilleboe's, asked us to watch their puppy for the weekend. Our house rule is "no sleepovers until the age of 8," but we made an exception for Jackson! He even shared!

Jackson and Tajah
it takes two
may 1998

"Thinking about our past and writing remembrances is therapeutic, and enlightening as well. In fact, in the process of recording remembrances, all sorts of feelings, visions, and hopes come to light."
—Charlotte Moss

We just want to . . .
RE
relax
rejuvenate
reassess
renew
reaffirm
rebel
reclaim
recline
recreate
reflect
refresh
release
retrace
reveal
revive

with NO restraint!

Nothing is better than time to spend, laughing and talking with you, my friend.

ture from each year can be chosen with all the important information from the year accompanying the photo.

Make a Who's Who Page

Family trees, friendship gardens, or picture collages are great ways to add many pictures of people on one page. Give the page a particular theme and document the who's who information and any other tidbits that would match the theme you have chosen.

Keep Any Itineraries from Trips to Show Your Location in the Photos

Itineraries or maps are helpful not only on a trip, but useful to recall the events at a later date. They can be kept in their original format or reduced on a copy machine (color or black and white) to support the storytelling of the event. When possible, use a small arrow sticker on the map to reference where you were when each picture was taken.

Reveal Your Inner Thoughts

Not everything you write must fall under the journalist questions: Who? What? Where? When? or Why? Revealing your feelings or inner thoughts can help you

recall the essence of the memory. Remember, your photos can show you where you were but they can't necessarily explain how you felt.

Interview Children Annually on Their Birthday

Ask them about their favorite happenings of the year, favorite memories, current best friends, and their goals for the future. You can also list teachers, subjects, sports, music, and other activities that they were involved in. Don't forget to measure their height and weight so they can chart their growth. They'll be surprised each year as they go back to read this information and discover how much things have changed or stayed the same.

creative ways to add journaling

Because journaling is so important to the way your pages tell their stories, here are some different ways to place the text on your pages in a creative fashion.

- Border the page with the beginning of the story, song, poem, or words that are befitting to the event.

- Caption stickers (custom made or preprinted) or caption cloud die cuts are two choices that can be used to create conversations on your pages.

- Let words fall where they may. Include applicable words or phrases in the background of a layout, either randomly or precisely for added definition of the theme.

- Create curved lines with templates, and journal in a wavy, jagged, or other interesting shaped line.

- Border the picture with pertinent information needed to identify who is in the photograph or what was happening.

- Die cuts add shape and word power. Use them to accentuate a theme or add journaling inside of them.

- Use your computer. Sometimes it is easier to tell a long story by typing it on the computer and reducing it down into the space available on the page. Be careful, this is addicting because it

Visiting Epcot in Florida always gives you plenty to do to amuse yourself. With an accompanying map, make notations on your layout where you were on the map when the picture was taken.

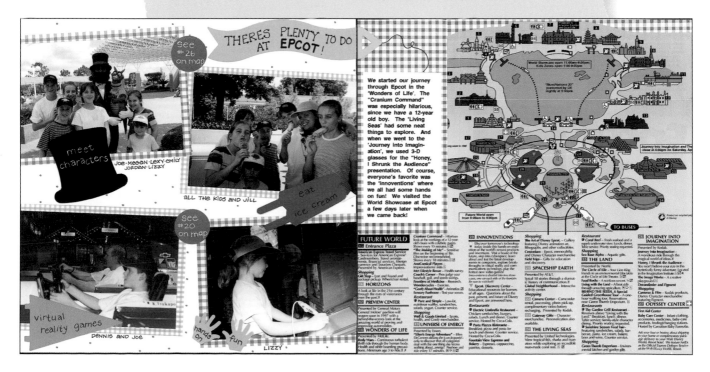

To the Falls

How We Got There!

Canada

New York

Michigan

LANSING - LEFT 4 am
NIAGARA - BY 9 am
ALBANY - BY 3 pm
DESTINATION CAPE - BY 7 pm

We left a rainy Michigan at 4 am and continued on up through Canada into Niagara Falls. It was cold and drizzly there too but that did not stop us from reveling in the beauty and wonder of the Falls. We didn't care anyway, we were two girls out on an adventure together!

To the Cape

The road to the Cape is long but familiar. There was plenty of time to daydream, sing, sight see, and anticipate all the fun we would experience. As we hit the Sagamore Bridge at the beginning of the Cape, we plugged the Yanni CD into the stereo and rolled down the windows (even though it was raining!) to smell the wonder of the sea air!

niagara falls
OUR FIRST STOP

CAPE

THE BAY SIDE

A week of...
laughing, singing, reminiscing, relaxing, discovering and just being!

THE OCEAN SIDE

After laying out your page design, the first stop should be to journal. Be sure to include details that will allow the reader to recreate the memory.

tends to look so much better than handwritten prose. However, it is very important for historical reasons to have your own penmanship throughout your scrapbook.

- Don't worry about not having perfect handwriting. Your ancestors will be thrilled that you recorded the information personally. So just write it down—ugly handwriting or not—before the memory is forgotten! You won't regret putting your personal touch on your scrapbook pages.

now is the time

Now is the time to get started, to share those details that bring your pictures to life. When Ronald Reagan was inaugurated as the 40th President of the United States he stated, "If not you, who? . . . if not now, when?" Even though I doubt that he was referring to photo journaling, he had a great point. Who else is going to share the magic of the stories that make up your fondest memories? Tell the story, your story, and add those wonderful details to your photographs before they are forgotten.

Frequently Asked Questions

Q: HOW CAN I DISPLAY THE WRITING ON THE BACK OF AN OLD PHOTO?

A: Sometimes the backs of old photographs contain priceless handwritten prose of those that have gone before. There are two simple ways to display this. For the easiest option, obtain a color copy of the back of the photo and mount it side by side, so both front and back can be viewed. Or, if you desire to see the actual writing on the photo, use a craft knife to carefully cut a "frame" in the paper the picture is to be mounted on so the writing can be viewed in its original form on the flip side of the page.

Q. WHAT CAN I DO WITH ITEMS THAT I WANT TO SAVE IN MY SCRAPBOOK BUT ARE TOO BIG OR DON'T REQUIRE JOURNALING?

A. Take a picture of the oversized item, put that in your scrapbook and dispose of the big item if desired. Journal the necessary information.

Q: I'M STUMPED! HOW DO I DECIDE WHAT TO WRITE?

A: Once you include the who, what, where, and when of your event, think about what you would say if you were relaying the story to a friend over lunch. Don't be afraid to "write" the story down. It may help to talk into a tape recorder, and then later, write down the condensed version, recording all of the important points.

Q: WHAT TYPE OF PENS SHOULD I USE FOR JOURNALING?

A: Use pens that are archival quality. It is most important for a pen to be permanent, lightfast, and waterproof to preserve the memories that you will record.

Q. I DON'T HAVE ANY PICTURES, BUT I WANT TO SHARE THIS EVENT IN MY SCRAPBOOK, NOT IN A PERSONAL JOURNAL. ANY IDEAS?

A: Yes! You can always go back and take "afterthought" pictures that can help document the event. For example, if you did not have pictures of the first day of school, go back and photograph the outside of the school, lay out the outfit you wore, and then add a story of your feelings from that first day. From an accident that was life changing, photograph the hospital you stayed in, return for photos of the professionals who cared for you, and then add the thoughts that make it all come together.

Creative Lettering

IT'S ALWAYS FUN TO LEARN OF SECRETS. Especially the kind of secrets that actually help you do something better. It's like discovering the mystery ingredient that you couldn't quite figure out in a secret recipe that has been closely guarded.

In this chapter I will share with you my secret for creative lettering. It will help you understand the concepts to perfect lettering—something we're all striving for on our pages. We'll also have a little fun with some creative styles that, hopefully, can get you started on inventing your own personal style. In addition, you'll learn the guidelines to making lettering look pleasing to your own eye and everyone else's!

IDAHO FALLS
APRIL 1998

EASTER FUN HUNT

The kids read clues that led them to a super treat at the end of the hunt. Everyone had a great time, especially Lizzy and Natalie (below).

It is so much more personal to have your own handwriting on a scrapbook page, especially when you are using products like pattern paper and stickers that are not your own original artwork. Write something on each page to make it more individual.

the secrets revealed

Most of us, at one time or another, have heard the three secrets to choosing real estate—location, location, and location. Which, of course, has lead everyone to come up with the strategy of learning any skill—practice, practice, and practice.

Well, that's all well and groovy, but if you don't understand the concepts of the game, how can you practice effectively? Practice only helps if you know what it is you're trying to do. If I sit down at the piano and play, I'm never going to play Beethoven unless someone teaches me which keys make which sounds and so forth. We must have direction.

I do not profess to be the master letterer or the end-all be-all of this great task. But I have been curious enough, coupled with a large dose of silly, to come up with a concept that I have taught to hundreds of people about creative lettering. The key is that it really works and it makes sense! Now there's a combination that is effective. Consider me the Dr. Laura of lettering!

Whenever I teach classes, I always like to tell a funny story, if not a downright

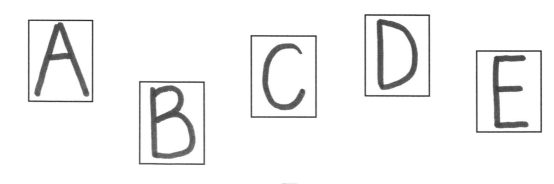

stupid one. I find it's much easier to re-member something "off the wall" later on than recall some run-of-the-mill infor-mation. So here's my story.

Back in the 70s, I remember seeing a movie called *The Stepford Wives* which starred Katherine Ross and had been written by the author Ira Levin (of *Rose-mary's Baby* fame). It was a story about a town somewhere in New England where the women were falling victim to a conspiracy. The men in the town had tainted the water with something that was making all the ladies turn almost ro-botic. They were slowly becoming the same (subservient, of course), and I be-lieve the goal was to make them perfect, well at least perfect in the way they wanted them to be. No one had any cel-lulite, everyone's house was clean, and they all started to look and act the same.

Have you started to wonder why I am telling you this? And what does this have to do with lettering? Well, all creative let-tering stems from a basic alpha-bet, all "Stepford" letters. They are in proportion with each oth-er, their size is the same, the midline for the letters is consis-tent, and there is similar harmo-ny among them. If the letters were in a box, they would each fit in the same one. Let's call this the "Stepford" box. No matter how the box size changes or if the midline gets moved up or down, they all conform to the same changes.

Creative lettering happens when we start to embellish the ba-sic letters, change the box size, mix letter sizes and styles, adjust the midline or vary it, and add decoration. But the basics remain the same and stay in harmony with

each other. Of course, there are always rules to bend, but these guidelines make up the backbone that makes your letter-ing look better. Then, once practice takes place, you will greatly improve, training your eye and hand to respond and letter with ease.

practice anywhere

The best part about practicing your let-tering is that you can do it anywhere! You could be on the phone and practice (this is officially called "doodling"), while waiting around for other people (while running carpool, waiting in a doc-tor's office, etc.) and the tools are not a nuisance to keep with you. It's not like trying to put a piano in your purse so

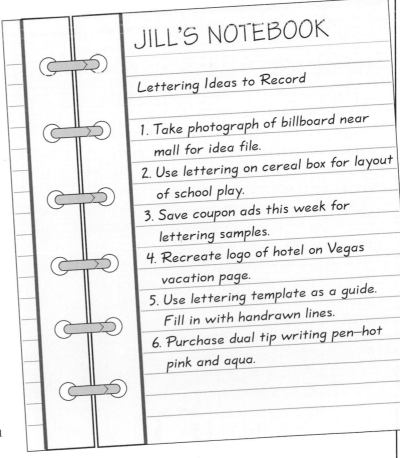

JILL'S NOTEBOOK

Lettering Ideas to Record

1. Take photograph of billboard near mall for idea file.
2. Use lettering on cereal box for layout of school play.
3. Save coupon ads this week for lettering samples.
4. Recreate logo of hotel on Vegas vacation page.
5. Use lettering template as a guide. Fill in with handrawn lines.
6. Purchase dual tip writing pen—hot pink and aqua.

Another Year Older & Better!
OCTOBER '98
jill turns 34!!

What a great day! Shopping, dinner out, chocolate cake, lots of presents, and being with the people I love! It doesn't get any better!

mmm-m extra double chocolate cake!

Lexig & me ... she's my angel girl!

opening my gift from Carole

Lizzy, Jill & Joe ... I love my kids!

me & Joe — my boy!

luggage from my Denny

When our ancestors review our scrapbooks in the future, they will want to see our own handwriting on the pages, rather than a computer font that was so handy in this technological age. There is no substitute for the handwritten word.

you can practice while you're running around town.

Also, a note about tools. Obviously, you need pens. There are a million different kinds out there, for a million different projects. For scrapbooking, at the very minimum, make sure your pens are acid-free. Ideally, choose pens that are archival that will not fade or smear. Practice on paper that is smooth, not lumpy or woven. And always have a clean eraser and ruler handy. These tools will help you get things precise, until you have practiced enough and are comfortable with "eyeballing it" on your own.

Begin by practicing the basic alphabet. Think about the "Stepford" box. Your inherent box size is the beginning of your personal style. Keep in mind that you will always have more control over your pen if you pull it towards you, rather than push it away. This means that the letter "M" is four lines, having lifted the pen as the line changes directions. This only applies to straight lines, not curved ones. Do not break the flow of an "O" or "U" or any other curved letter. Remember, if your basic alphabet isn't perfected, then when you embellish your letters with different techniques, those letters can look jumbled and messy.

After you become proficient with the basic alphabet, you will be ready to begin embellishing. Remember, if the basics aren't mastered, then when you go to embellish, it can look like your dog did it.

Aa a Bb Cc Dd Ee
Ff Gg Hh Ii Jj
Kk Ll Mm Nn
Oo Pp Qq Rr Ss
Tt t Uu u Vv Ww
Xx Yy y Zz

the basic alphabet

Sit up straight. Also, keep your paper straight and parallel with your writing surface. This way you can actually see if you are writing straight or not. Do not put your paper on a diagonal, unless you are writing cursive.

**Step One:
Use Pencil**

**Step Two:
Outline**

**Step Three:
Erase Pencil**

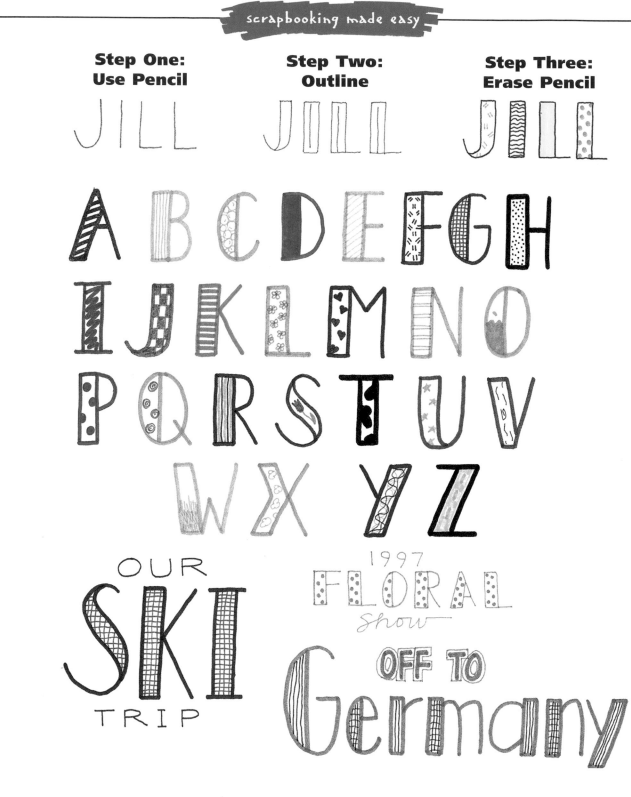

fill-in letters

Practice your basic alphabet on lined notebook paper or grid paper. Practice within three lines, using the second line as the midline for the letters.

adding embellishments

Place serif and embellishment lines in the opposite direction of the line on the letter. Vertical lines need a horizontal serif. On a diagonal line, place serif on a diagonal for more visual interest.

outlining

When mixing upper and lowercase letters (making them all the same height) a good standard is making the vowels lowercase. Some consonants look cuter in lowercase, like the "N." Just be consistent throughout your lettering.

Step One:
Use Pencil

Step Two:
Outline

Step Three:
Erase Pencil

Try it   Try it   Try it

Aa Bb Cc Dd Ee
Ff Gg Hh Ii Jj
Kk Ll Mm Nn Oo
Pp Qq Rr Ss Tt
Uu Vv Ww Xx
Yy Zz

block letters

Remember, spacing is important. If you want the letters to overlap, keep them closer together. If you do not want them to overlap, allow space between each basic letter to accommodate the embellishment.

A B C D E F G H I J
K L M N O P Q R S
T U V W X Y Z

Note: Depending on where you want your shadow to be, outline the letter either on the right and bottom side <u>or</u> the left and top side.

SCARY SCREAMIE
HALLO-WEENIE

MELVIN

★ MY FIRST TOOTH

Scrapbook USA

high noon letters

Do not keep a death grip on your pen. This tires out your hand, causing shakiness and ruining your pen nib. Hold your pen with a soft, but firm grip.

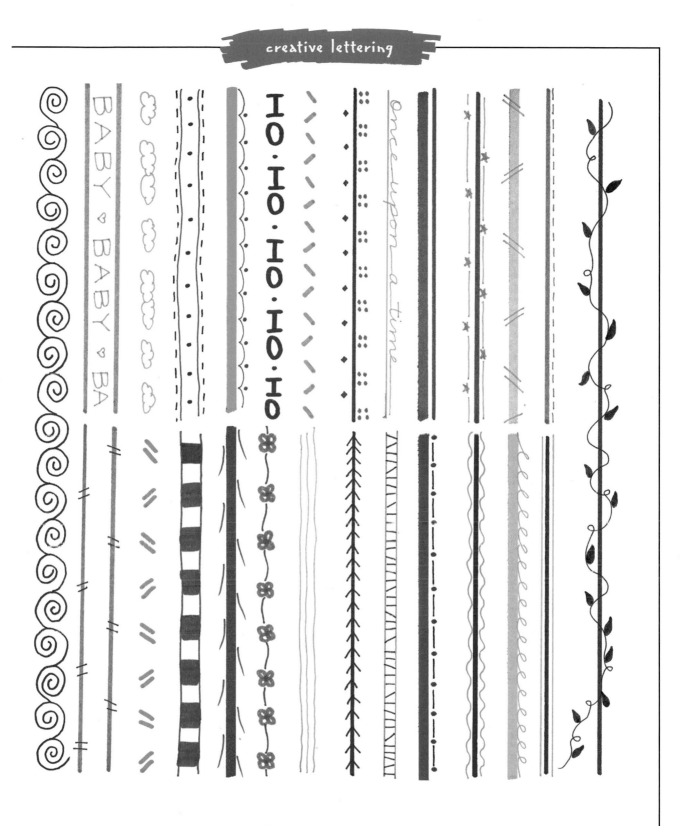

borders

If you are stuck with a tight spot to put lettering in, use a pencil and place the middle letter or word from the phrase in the middle of the space. Add the other letters left and right to make sure the words get centered correctly.

using different pen tips

Store paint markers and dual-tip pens flat, with single-tip pens stored vertically in a cup, nib side down, to keep the ink in the pen tip. Purchase a variety of different pen tips for lettering diversity.

go ahead, try it

Now that you know the secrets, you can use your creativity to invent your own artistic fonts. When you think of a style you'd like to try, write out the entire alphabet. You will then see how the letters that look similar are embellished in harmony with one another. This also will serve as a handy reference guide for you later, as you build up a nice collection of font ideas for future projects.

To create your own font, simply put on your thinking cap and choose a theme or design that matches your project. Let's use a swirl as an example. Will it merely be drawn over each letter or incorporated into its line? Next, whatever you do to one straight line should be done to the next in each letter. If you decide to change the curved line of a letter in a certain fancy way, then change each curved line of every letter. Letters at the beginning and ending of a word can be embellished and exaggerated for added flourish, while leaving the middle letters plain or toned down.

persist in doing

There's a quote that states, "That which we persist in doing becomes easier for us to do; not that the nature of the thing itself has changed, but that our power to do is increased." I think the author was Emerson, and he must have been fabulous at creative lettering if that was his interest! Persist in doing, and the more you practice, the better you will become. In no time, you will be able to look at that scrapbook layout and wonder, "Who did that fabulous lettering?" and then the answer will come to you, "Oh, yeah, that was me!"

Purchasing Pens

You should purchase acid-free, permanent, archival pens in a variety of tips. Always buy basic black in all pen tips you prefer to work with. Thin markers, used for outlining and detail, really make a difference in creative lettering. Other than black, I recommend gold, silver, and white (invaluable for writing on dark papers) for additional basics in your tool box. Brown is an attractive neutral color that looks especially rich with vintage photos. Beyond these basics, you should choose a palette of colors that coincide with the themes of most of your pictures.

Frequently Asked Questions

Q: HOW CAN I GET OVER THE THOUGHT THAT MY HANDWRITING ISN'T "GOOD ENOUGH" TO PUT ON MY PAGES?

A: Imagine that you were just given a diary that belonged to your great-great grandmother, who you were named after. It contains her feelings, clues of her lifestyle, her innermost thoughts, and history. You feel connected to her, even closer to her, knowing that even though more than a century has passed between the time she lived and when you were born, you are very much the same. Are you now thinking, "Gee, her handwriting is kinda sloppy"? What's up with her lack of perfection and cuteness with her lettering? Of course you aren't thinking that. It would be silly. Someday your ancestors won't care either.

Q: WHAT DO I DO IF I MAKE A MISTAKE?

A: Fix it, of course. Cover it up with an embellishment or another piece of paper with your corrected lettering on it. Or you could purchase acid-free correction tape to match your background color.

Q: CAN I USE CRAYONS IN MY SCRAPBOOK?

A: You can use anything, but I wouldn't use crayons if I were you. The wax from the crayons is not the best thing to have near your photos. Use colored pencils or markers instead.

Q: WHAT TYPE OF PENS SHOULD I BUY?

A: Purchase pens that are lightfast, fade-proof, and permanent. Buy colors that will match the ones you use most, or just stick with basic black.

Q: HOW CAN I MAKE MY WRITING LOOK ITS BEST?

A: First, with a pencil, give yourself a line guide to write on, so you aren't writing uphill. Second, use a pen with a clean tip (not frayed or running out of ink). Now, sit up straight, put your pen to paper, and go for it!

Terrific Titles

Picture the Academy Awards. It's the final award and everyone awaits breathlessly for its announcement. The ever-chic, slender celebrity smiles and states, "And the winner for Best Picture goes to . . . (envelope ripping) . . . the story about the boat that sank in cold ocean waters after hitting an iceberg!" Huh!?!

What's in a title? And where would we be without them? These are some of the questions we will answer in this chapter. I will show you how a title does make a difference, how to choose one, where to place it, and all you need to know to make those title pages extra special!

"hey, you"

We all have titles, whether we want to admit it or not. Our given names are a title. Just try calling your children without one ("Hey, blond one!) or attempt to call a place of business and try to actually get the person you want to talk to on the phone. ("Can I talk to the guy in that department that makes those things?")

Titles are a good thing. They help us locate the video, song, or book we might be looking for. Without them, there would be chaos and a lot of wasted time trying to locate people or items we need.

Check out the difference in the sample page layouts below. What's missing from the left one? The colors and the photos are the same, and the journaling seems fine. However, one crucial thing is different: without a title, the focus is gone.

more power to ya!

If words give power, then a title can be the main muscle for any written prose. A title brings focus to your scrapbook page; it's the first impression for your memory. In just a few short words, the entire feeling of an event can be summed up.

A Title Should Do One of 3 Things

1. GIVE INFORMATION
2. CONVEY A FEELING
3. CREATE INTEREST

Looking at pictures is fun, but it can get boring quickly without the words to give it personality. The title sets the stage for the feeling of the story. Hoola Hoop and trampoline jumping may never be Olympic events, but it's always fun to dream.

A title can do all three things as shown here: give information, convey a feeling, and create interest. Holy Cow! Just a few words and you've changed the world (well . . . at least the layout).

A Title Should Give Information

It can be as simple as "Boston 1988," "Fall Days 1996," or "First Haircut." When putting information in a title, it's best to get right to the point and keep it simple.

Choose To Convey a Feeling in the Form of a Title

Remember that many interesting words and phrases can be chosen to convey the desired feeling in your title. This can be as simple as one word. For example, "Ouch!" "Super!" or "Mine!" immediately leads us to the feelings of something that hurt, a job well done or toddler selfishness among playmates. A feeling was created and the foundation set for the rest of the story.

Phrases can do the same, serving as the beginning of a story you wish to tell. "How Do I Love Thee . . ." "No Greater Joy . . ." or "Superstar Athlete!" are titles that beg for more information. The key is to keep the reader's interest. They want to know more, and you've got them hooked through the feeling!

Your Title Should Convey Interest

This leads us to the third concept of creating interest. "Once upon a time . . ." has always been the classic opening for a story, but can also serve as a title for a scrapbook page. With the title, you want to pique an interest. With just enough words to interest your reader, you can add the excitement and intrigue in a title that will help create the focus of your layout and the basis for the story to come. The title "Holy Cow! I'm Getting My Ears Pierced!" that I used on a page about my daughter not only created a focus for the layout (the cow print), gave information (getting ears pierced), and conveyed a feeling (holy cow, the pain was a surprise!), but created curiosity about the rest of the story.

While remembering these three points, you can easily choose titles to give your scrapbook pages the focus they need. Although you may find some ideas to inspire you in books that give you title samples, you won't need to be dependent on someone else's title version of an event. Draw upon your memory with these three simple points and choose a title that will fasci-

OUR FIRST WINTER

After a lifetime in Southern California, Mom and Dad spent their first real winter in Salt Lake City, Utah in December 1997. At last, an excuse to buy more winter clothes!

There's a first time for everything, no matter how old you are! So, you've had your last time to make a page without a title. A title creates the focus needed to recall a special memory of the past.

the feeling? Then convey that feeling through the title. Did something interesting or out of the ordinary happen? Then use your title to create that interest.

give it a title

If you don't give it a title, someone else will! And it may be . . . BORING! While reading information

nate your reader into wanting to know more about your wonderful memories!

To decide which of the 3 points is best for your layout, ask yourself this question:

WHAT WAS THE MOST IMPORTANT PART OF THE MEMORY?

Just the fact of what it was? Go with an information title. Was it

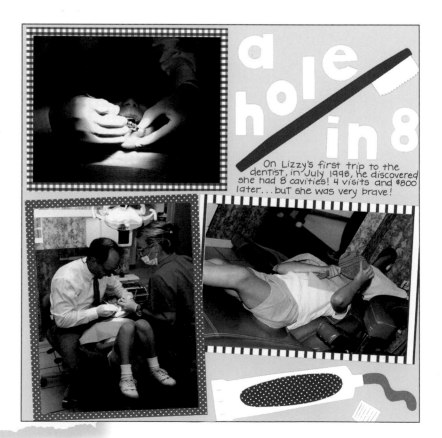

a hole in 8

On Lizzy's first trip to the dentist, in July 1998, he discovered she had 8 cavities! 4 visits and $800 later...but she was very brave!

Going to the dentist can be pretty boring (no offense, Dr. Watts). So give your page a title that will give the same shock your mother had when she found out you had eight cavities! There goes the scrapbooking budget for the month.

Even mundane activities, like having a piano delivered, can be exciting with the right title and layout. Titles can bring excitement to your page, so let the scrapbooking begin!

located on a scrapbook page (hopefully the who, what, where, and why of what happened), the person examining your pictures and journaling may draw their own conclusion as to what the event was about. Now, I realize this may not seem like a life-or-death situation, but you can be sure that if I take the time to scrapbook a memory, I want it to have the correct information—feeling and all! Remember, scrapbooking is a personal history and should be as accurate as possible. So unless you have the pictures and the tattoo to prove it, no one is going to buy the fact that you may have had a short fling in college with Harrison Ford.

the historical facts of a photograph.

Use your title to begin telling the story of the memory. In Chapter 3, we discussed creative ways to give information to your pictures. The title you choose acts as the jumping off point for your storytelling.

everybody needs somebody

If everybody needs somebody, then titles and journaling are a couple. The title is only half the story and should not be an excuse for not adding the most important words to your pictures—the photo journaling. Although a great title can give information and and pique interest, it's the details of your pictures that make the true difference. The who and when are particularly important for establishing

high and low

If you are now wondering where to get help finding titles, your search is over. There are many places to find inspiration for titles. A few good places to go to find titles for scrapbook pages are the following:

Video Store

Need I say more? Who has more titles than these people? Go ahead and browse the aisles for ideas.

Don't fall over from exhaustion trying to find the right title for your page. It can be as easy as one descriptive word that can sum up the entire event, pronto!

Movie Guide Book

Like to "steal" your titles in private? A small investment can be made in a movie guide book that lists every movie title ever made. Most of these are paperback and very inexpensive.

Book Store

Why reinvent the wheel? Walk down the aisle of the subject you are scrapbooking (garden, babies, etc.) and get plenty of ideas for your pages. Don't forget your notepad or Dictaphone.

TV Guide

Same as a movie guide with new ideas weekly!

Thesaurus

Look up a word that has something to do with the event and find

There's no fun like title fun, and scrapbookers "just wanna have fun." Put some enthusiasm into your titles with a few words that rhyme.

Waiting for Spring

March 1997

It was a cold winter like any other, but Lizzy and Jackson were getting anxious for those long, lazy days that begin in spring. The grass and the woods beyond were beckoning them, but they would still have to wait for the pleasures that come in Spring.

The title of this page brings the emotion and meaning to the photograph that is not necessarily apparent to the image.

more gratifying and fulfilling words to use for your title (see, I use mine too!)

Title Idea Books

These books have been compiled with you in mind. Usually they are laid out with themes, titles, quotes and scriptures, and they are organized in a handy reference guide format.

Music

Check out your CD collection or think of your favorite lullaby or hymn for title and/or phrase ideas.

Tantalizing Title Ideas

Play on words
From "Hair" to Eternity
Havin' a "Berry" Good Time
One in a "Melon"
"Sea's" the Day

One liner's
Got . . . (Spirit, Nerve, Tickets, or Diapers)??
Don't Go There!
How Nice for You
The Real (San Francisco, Dallas, New York, Orlando) Treat

Inspirational
Living. Loving. Laughing.
Know peace? Know the Cape.
Sisters by Chance. Friends by Choice.

Slang Terms
Gettin' Jiggy
Bustin' a Move
Gotta . . . (Dance, Jam or Play)!
Ain't Nothin' like . . .
Gonna Get Me Some . . .

The I's have it
I Love You Because . . .
I Wish, I Hope, I Dream for . . .
I Love to . . .
I Remember When . . .
I Can't Believe We . . .

Single Page Layout Ideas

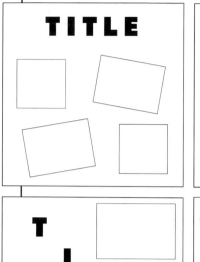

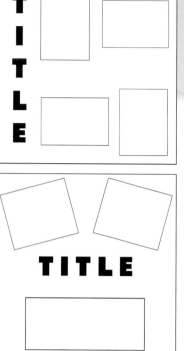

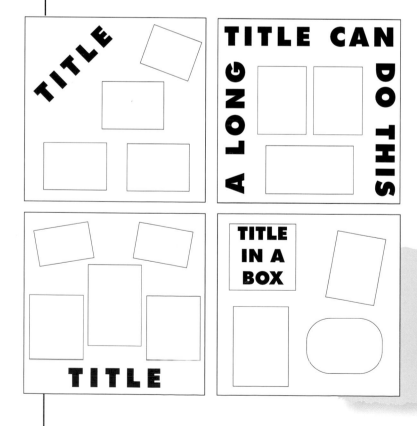

A title can be placed in many different ways on your layout, just make sure:

1. It's big enough to be noticed immediately
2. No words are misspelled, unless on purpose (usually for emphasis)
3. It's legible (not perfect, just legible)

The Yellow Pages

Use the Yellow Pages as a reference guide for titles. Look up a subject and find new ideas from the advertisements and business names listed under that heading. There are usually many different ideas to choose from and these catchy names and phrases can make great titles

Your Brain

I know this sounds like a long stretch, but thinking of the memory may actually make something pop into your head! Wouldn't that just be cool?!

where to put it

Now that you have come up with your title, where does it go? A title

Titles can be made from:

1. Creative hand lettering
2. Sticker letters or phrases
3. An alphabet template traced directly on the scrapbook page or onto different paper and then cut out.

These two types of titles (extending across two pages) draw your eye out and across the layout, hinting that there must be more to look at. Consequently, these are good for layouts of more than just two pages.

can be displayed many different ways on your page. It will add not only real content but visual interest to your layout as well. It can be executed many ways, but let's cover effective placement. Of course, titles do not have to be placed straight to be effective. In fact, that can be dull. Add visual emphasis by placing titles:

- On a curved line
- Within a shape
- With letters scattered or jumping
- Surrounded by matting
- As individual letters or words on die cut shapes
- Bordering a page

Try to use your own creative lettering whenever possible in your titles. This type of lettering makes the title more personal because it is written in your own hand.

These two examples are best if your layout only consists of two pages. The one above keeps your eye pulled inward while the one below hints "this is it" with the title continuing until the end of the layout.

Double Page Layout Ideas

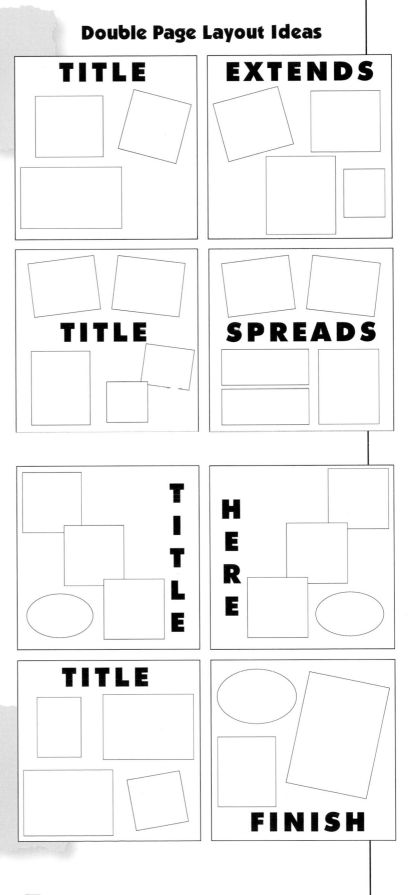

BAHAMAS

SeaEscape
FLORIDA
02.14.97
FORT LAUDERDALE

FEBRUARY 1997

CRUISIN' ALONG

We started our trip out by flying to Florida where we met up with Trent and Kelley Tenney, our close friends who live in Utah. We spent the night in a hotel then bright and early the next morning we boarded the cruise ship that would take us on a six hour cruise to the Bahamas. A buffet was served and plenty of fruit drinks offered, music played, and enough reasons given to get

The beaches in the Bahamas were beautiful. The water was warm and turquoise color with the sand a light contrast of fine taupe colored grains. We roamed by the pool daily and walked along the beach. We rented a jet ski for an hour one day, and Dennis and I had a blast! Kelley relaxed on shore while we jumped and surfed the waves. It was pretty choppy that day on the water.

After our days of playing in the warm sun, we rested and renewed ourselves for a fabulous dinner every night in a different restaurant on the island. One night while we ate, we watched from the balcony as sharks swam below us for their nightly feeding. There were about forty of them in a frenzy. It was an interesting sight! As always, there was much laughter and fun with Trent and Kelley and Dennis and I. Kelley and I even got to show off for our sunblock! This truly was a trip to remember!

Dennis, Jill, Kelley & Trent

The restaurant where the sharks are fed nightly in the bay.

AHHH SUPPERTIME!

OLD FRIENDS BEST FRIENDS!

SNORKELING

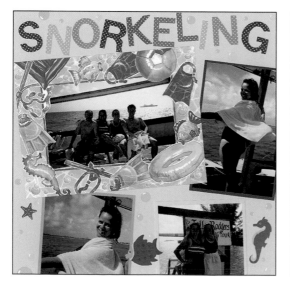

We took a boat out to a beautiful area where an underwater corral reef filled with sea life awaited us. With our rented fins and masks, we plunged into the warm water where we saw colorful fishes and flowing sea plants on the ocean's floor. We fed and swam with the fishes. What a snorkeling adventure!

subtitles

Subtitles are secondary titles used within a scrapbook layout of more than three pages that explain or highlight a change in the activity. The easiest way to explain this is to show you. See the samples on the previous two pages. These pages are the entire layout for a trip to the Bahamas. As can see, each segment that changes with a new subtitle is emphasizing a new activity. Although "Bahamas" is the title that could umbrella the entire story, the subtitles bring new meaning to each arrangement of photos.

Subtitles are best used when you are scrapbooking an event that will include several pages. They can be classified with a new activity, a change in feeling or setting, or a switch in location.

COMMUNICATES WITH THE RIGHT WORDS AND PHRASES

- Subtitles—used to define a change in activity or feeling
- Journaling—gives the important details of the story
- Closing Comments—wrap up the feelings of an event in a few words or less

Choose a title that will make a statement about the story you are telling. A title will be your chance to make a first impression, to plant a thought, and to help a particular memory come to life. Remember . . . create, capture, and communicate your feelings through a well chosen title.

the 3 c's of choosing a title

CREATES FOCUS

- Gives information about the event
- Shares a feeling that remains with the memory
- Creates more interest for a particular recollection

CAPTURES ATTENTION

- With interesting placement on your page
- Through proper execution in the layout, taking into account the total number of pages used
- By using variety in placement, execution, and content

JILL'S NOTEBOOK

Title Ideas

Two Less Lonely People in the World—from old Air Supply song (use on engagement pages)

Our Trip to "Sa-cago" (Chicago)—that's how Lizzy pronounced it!

Hoops on Fire (from MSU ads)—use on basketball pages for Joe

Living Juicy (from book by SARK)—use with pictures of something that was fabulously fun and indulgent!

When giving your layouts titles, keep the mood of the event in mind. For a more serious and respectful frame of mind, such as visiting an historical monument, an informational title exudes the respect the memorial deserves.

frankly my dear . . .

Every good scrapbook story deserves a great beginning and an even better ending. Actually, so does every chapter in a book, (so I'm sweating it out here to come up with something fabulous for my closing comments!).

Thomas Jefferson once stated, "The ultimate power lies in the people themselves. If you think them not enlightened to cast an informed discretion, the remedy is not to take away their discretion . . . but simply inform it." Consider yourself informed, and get to work! A great title will be the essence of getting off to a great start!

Frequently Asked Questions

Q: DOES EVERY PAGE NEED A TITLE?

A: No, not every page. However, when the location or subject changes in your layout, there should be a new title to help the reader understand that a change has occurred and inform him or her of the necessary details. Depending on how you scrapbook (one continuous timeline or "story" form with various events), a title can add meaningful focus to your layouts.

Q: IF I GET STUMPED, HOW CAN I THINK OF TITLES?

A: Think of the event. What comes to mind? Look around for catchy phrases that make you remember the particular details of the event.

Q: HOW LARGE SHOULD I MAKE MY TITLE?

A: Large enough to notice it's the title, but not so large that it detracts from the pictures. First consider the space needed for photos, then earmark room for a title and embellishments.

Q: WON'T JUST ONE BIG TITLE PAGE AT THE FRONT OF THE SCRAPBOOK SUFFICE?

A: If your book is an overview of your entire life (or a portion of it) in a nutshell, then you can begin with a full title page (i.e., The Life and Times of Jane Doe). Even so, your layouts will benefit from subtitles used to give information or create a feeling or focus.

Q: IF A TITLE SAYS IT ALL, DO I STILL NEED TO JOURNAL?

A: Yes, at least with the minimum of who, when, and where.

Q: WHAT PRODUCTS SHOULD I USE TO CREATE MY TITLE?

A: There are many products out there: stickers, markers, ABC templates, computer fonts, and even ready-made titles in many forms. If using a ready-made title, be sure it shows your personality and conveys your message. If not, be confident and make your own.

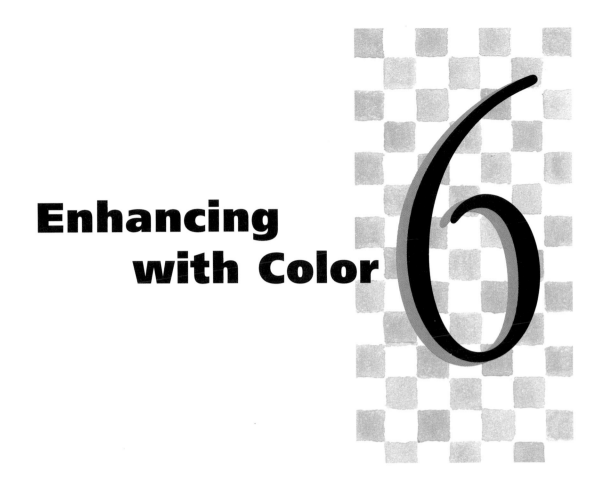

Enhancing with Color 6

COLOR HAS POWER. COLOR IS MEMORY. Color creates mood, lifts spirits, evokes fear and, at times, shouts "Look at me!" Color jars memories, strengthening our association with things of the past—like the plum-colored, matching dresses my mother made for me and my sister, nine years my senior, when I was eight years old. Although the styles were different, the colors brought us together, two sisters sharing a color palette.

In this chapter, you will learn how to choose the colors that will not only make your pictures look their best and enhance the focus of your page, but that will also make your memories come alive!

FL☀RIDA
April '97

Over spring break, me and the kids flew down to Florida. We met up with our friends the Schneiders. Dennis flew in from business in Palm Springs. And Jackson and Molly stayed home and went to puppy camp together!

The clan infront of the Hard Rock Cafe in Orlando

Hard Rock CAFE

The first night there, we ate dinner at the 'Kingdom of Rock and Roll', which is right outside Universal Studios. Over dinner, the Schneider's told us they would be moving to Germany this summer. We were sad about that but excited about the trip ahead of us and the fun we would have!

Left to Right-Top:
Robbie, Megan, Lexy, Lyndon, & Emily
Bottom: Jordan, Joe, Lizzy & Jill

With Florida in mind, one cannot help but think of the colors of bright sunlight and water. These summer hues helped to create the exciting mood that was enjoyed throughout the trip.

understanding color's effects

There's nothing truer than the fact that color creates mood. Color stimulates the memory, sending signals to the brain. Alexandra Stoddard in her *Book of Color* explains, "By relating colors to memories, you train your eye to envision those special moments that have delighted you, and you will always react honestly to color."

What a fabulous realization this is for the art of scrapbooking! Through this art, we are trying to preserve those precious memories of our lives. Knowing that color can actually help stimulate memory gives great power to us, the artists. Color is an intimate reference of your life. Keep in touch with how you react to it emotionally because

When I created my scrapbook page, I blatantly copied the entire color scheme and design of the logo from this famous tourist site to keep the memory rockin' on.

this can give you meaningful clues toward your color choices for your layouts.

No matter how much you are taught about color, no one can tell you which colors will speak to you. You may be the only one available to convey to future generations, through your choice of color, what the moment felt like. Color will help you personalize your memories even more.

remembering color

We all have recollections of color that vividly evoke the memories that make up our life. I remember the baby blue bedspreads in the bedroom I shared with my sister Jan, the black and white uniforms (and later green) that my brother wore all his years of football, and the rust-colored uniform my oldest sister, Joy, wore to work the year she was a waitress and made enough money to buy me a pink Barbie Dream House for Christmas! I was nine at the time, and color was very much a part of my life then. Color is still a part of my memories now.

I used bright colors for these pages to imitate the visual smorgasbord found at Disney World. The background pattern I used for these pages was chosen to match Minnie's dress.

Scientists are now discovering the link between color and memory, believing that color sends signals to the brain. These signals help us recall what has already passed—and isn't that what scrapbooking is all about? Expressing color symbolically becomes our autobiography! Remember, by relating color to memories, we train our eye to envision those special moments that have delighted us. Color brings power to our fingertips!

With this influence, you can create or enhance a memory. Think of a vacation you have taken. Where was it spent? On a sandy, beige beach with turquoise blue water, or in a lively city where festivals showcase the wild colors on ruffled skirts on a dance floor? Was it spent in a city with gray buildings and concrete everywhere, or in the woods with towering pine trees creating an evergreen sky above and brown bark extending down to the earth? Each of these examples have very distinct color references. Didn't you picture in your mind that you were there, amid those colors, when you read the examples?

The best aid to help us remember the color of an event is color film. That color memory has been locked into your photo and, with proper care, will remain as a testament of color in your life. It is our job, as the scrapbook artist, to bring intensity to the page and stimulate the memories that exist. It is important to keep in mind that the colors we add to our scrapbook page should always enhance the photograph and never detract from it or compete with it. With this thought, we can choose colors that will create a backdrop for the feelings or mood we had the first time around.

Nature's colors (the browns and greens) were chosen for this layout because they are part of the memory of this trip to the great outdoors. The pine tree die cuts were folded in half and run through a crimping tool to add texture to the trees.

ISLAND PARK, IDAHO
MaY 1992

DENNIS·JILL·BABY LIZZY CUDDLING

LEXY·DENNIS·JOE ENJOY THE OUTDOORS

LEXY·DENNIS·JOE ON THE 4-WHEELER

JOE·JILL·LIZZY·LEXY

JILL·LIZZY INFRONT OF THE HARRIS CABIN

color associations

Remember that colors will always produce different feelings and moods. It is important to ensure that your color choice reflects the feelings and mood that you want for your page. Also, remember that colors are representative of common things.

Red

Red is a stimulating and powerful color. Red puts an exclamation mark on pages and is a self-confident color that begs to be noticed. Use red in small doses, unless you want it to exude the boldness and fun of the event.

Feelings Created	Common Uses
high energy	flowers
danger/warning	hearts
strength	fruit
passion	picnics
warmth/heat	school days
courage	parties
durability	fire

Yellow

Yellow is happy and healthy and is associated with the sun and warmth. It adds light and can make dark pictures look their best. Yellow is a welcoming color, and it can liven your spirits. Use yellow in its clearest form, from a primary yellow to pastels and a soft hue I call butter yellow. Stay away from yellows that are darkened by green or black, they may make photographs look chemically washed out.

Feelings Created	Common Uses
happiness	sunflowers
brightness	lemons
excitement	sunshine
hope	spring time
kindness	school supplies
joy	baby chicks
generosity	beach gear

Purple

Purple is the color of royalty and richness. It adds a depth of feeling and feels perfumed. Purple has often been labeled as a feminine color, but in reality, men, women, boys, and girls all look great with purple. Pastel purple and yellow is my favorite combination, and in darker shades, it reminds me of the L.A. Lakers. Purple adds life and mystery. Many people are afraid to use purple, but it can be used freely in a variety of ways. Purple is an excellent accent color.

Blue

Blue is cool and serene, relaxes the mind and brings peace. It is the sign of victory (first place ribbons). It also can mean sadness (feeling blue). Use blue to recall peaceful feelings. Blue is universal and can be used in its various shades anywhere. Blue can accentuate a colder temperature (such as a snow scene) and can bring balance to the warmth of a beach layout (sun and water). Blue is a working color and is flattering for almost everything and everyone.

Feelings Created	Common Uses
mysterious	magicians
distinction	balloons
youthful	flowers
relaxation	Easter
friendship	kids
unity	babies (pastel)
spontaneity	candy

Feelings Created	Common Uses
patriotism	water
peace	sky
sensitivity	denim
sadness	nautical
honor	sea life
winning	nighttime
serenity	flowers

Green

Green is restful and considered a basic color (think of nature—almost everything is green). It can mean jealousy (we are green with envy) and denotes knowledge. It is the color of fertility, growth, and balance. It is the earth's color. Green relaxes and heals, and it improves concentration. Since green is a basic color, use it freely to bring forth the colors of nature in your photos. Layer various shades of green to add depth and dimension to natural backgrounds. Use green freely, enhancing nature and bringing it alive.

Orange

Orange is strong and vital and is the color of youth. Orange adds drama and depth. Peach is a very flattering shade of orange and is better used for photographs of older people, whereas bright orange is wonderful for children and young adults. Orange adds fun. Orange is a very vibrant color and can easily steal the show, as its neighbor red often does. Use orange to accent feelings of excitement and energy.

Feelings Created	Common Uses
healing	leaves
living	money
growing	frogs
progress	reptiles
knowledgeable	grass
dependable	vegetables
safety	earth

Feelings Created	Common Uses
happy	pumpkins
fresh	sunshine
energetic	Halloween
witty	sports
charming	autumn
glowing	garden pots
security	popsicles

other crisp colors in balancing photos that have too much light in them. Black is best used as an accessory. Black is a pirate flag, penguins, insects, asphalt, cameras, binoculars, a witch, a cat, a bat, a cauldron, tuxedos, a chalkboard, and a graduation cap.

Metallic Gold, Silver, or Copper

Metallic gold, silver, or copper add reflection and symbolize success (a pot of gold, a silver lining, the brass ring). Metallics are a striking addition to any color and are great as an accessory or as the primary focus. Metallic pens are an excellent addition to anyone's scrapbook tool box (Marvy, Metallic Gel Rollers are my favorite). Metallics can be used to represent coins, jewelry, ornaments, tools, cars, airplanes, buses, trains, buttons, zippers, building structures, kitchen utensils, silverware, bikes, musical instruments, keys, glitter, anniversaries and weddings, chains, bells, picture frames, treasure, lightning, trophies, boat accessories, medical instruments, sports equipment, scissors, and stars.

White

White is pure and heavenly and virtuous and clean. White represents inner light and enhances all true colors. All photos look good around white. White is an excellent choice to use with another color when double framing your photos. White represents clouds, baseballs, angels, volleyballs, a bath tub, a dog bone, a picket fence, teeth, snow, chalk, and pure linen.

Brown

Brown is muddy and should be used in small doses with photos, otherwise they may look darker than desired. Tan or beige is the best color to use for brown because it represents the earth tones without darkening the others. Brown represents chocolate, wood, our dog Jackson, a football, dirt, a baseball mitt, a picnic basket, sand, horses, shopping bags, acorns, bark, pretzels, cola, and autumn leaves.

Black

Black is mysterious and often signifies death or mourning. Black darkens photos and can be used to your advantage with

the color wheel

There are three primary colors: red, yellow and blue. They cannot be obtained by mixing other colors together. These are the colors that make up every color in the rainbow, in various shades, tints, and tones. The secondary colors—the ones between the primary colors—are orange, green, and purple. These are created by mixing equal parts of their neighboring primary colors. These are the colors that are pictured on the color wheel. You probably learned these in

The Color Wheel

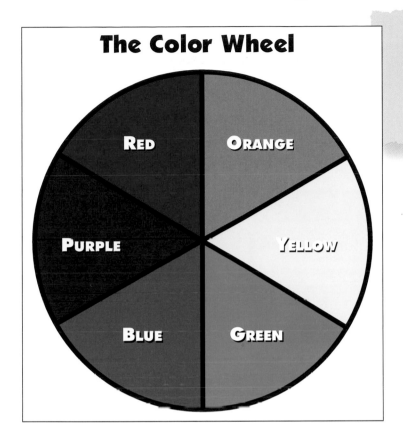

The color wheel shows the relationship between the primary colors (red, blue, and yellow) and the secondary colors (orange, purple, and green). Colors next to and directly across from each other are the complimentary colors.

quently turn into colors we consider pastel. Adding black to a color will darken it, creating a shade of that color. Black added to green becomes hunter green and creates in the other colors what we generally refer to as "jewel" colors.

A tone is created when gray (equal parts of black and white) is added, lessening the intensity of the color. If photos are too light, using color shades (provided they fit the mood) can help

school as ROYGBIV (red, orange, yellow, green, blue, indigo, violet), I've often thought that was funny, but I've always remembered it.

You can expand your color palette (creating variations of the primary colors) by adding different amounts of white, black, or gray to these basic colors. Use these variations to give uniformity to your page.

White added to a color creates a tint of that color. White added to red becomes pink, and all other colors subse-

The color palette shows the different variations that can be created by adding white or black. The center column represents the colors from the color wheel, with their variations on either side. Notice how your eye flows vertically from the shades to the basics to the tints.

The Color Palette

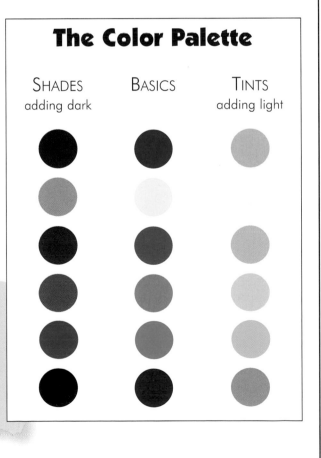

SHADES adding dark	BASICS	TINTS adding light

Working Colors

Choose colors that will enhance the mood of your memories.

Babies: pastel pink, violet, blue and yellow

Kids: primary (red, yellow, and blue), brights (hot pink, purple, lime green, turquoise and royal blue)

Vintage: neutrals (cream, black, brown, and oatmeal), jewels (dark green, wine, navy and gold), pastels (gray, stone blue, hyacinth)

Teens: bold (black, white, berry pink, orange, lime and purple)

Weddings: tone on tone (cream and/or white with touches of mauve, lavender, moss green, and butter yellow)

Vacations: serene (sand, celedon blue, sky), fun (red, blue, purple, orange, yellow), nature (oatmeal, forest green, slate blue, and moss green)

When choosing colors for a layout, consider the event subject and the age of the people shown in your photographs. Use the colors that were popular during the time your photos were taken.

balance the depth on the page. When photos are dark, choose lighter pastels or bright colors to add light to your page. Stay within the same color palette (shades, basics, or tints) to keep color harmony on your page so it doesn't detract your eye from the focus.

choosing color

• As a general rule for keeping colors as a backdrop to your photos rather than allowing them to become the focus, use the same tint or shade of all the colors you

If your photographs don't possess the eye-popping color you feel will set the mood of the layout, utilize those in your choice of background paper and embellishments. Your color choices should be in harmony with your title.

put on one page. If you start with one pastel, add another pastel color to keep the harmony of your layout. When the colors compete for attention, they detract from the real focal point of your scrapbook—your photos!

- However, when using a background paper that has a mix of tints and shades, match any accessory colors to the background as closely as possible, staying away from any colors that are too dominant for the mood of the event.

- All colors match their neighboring color on the color wheel. The color opposite them on the color wheel is also always a match.

Except for the black and red, the colors of this page reflect the exuberant celebration we had at Disney World. The red and black are too shocking for my chosen color scheme but were used to reflect my mood at the time—my camera breaking on vacation just when I needed it most.

- Resist asking other people for advice on color choices. Remember, you must determine the mood and feeling you want to add to your page depending upon the mood and feeling from the actual event. Refer to the color association section of this book for color mood ideas.

- Each page should have a color scheme, creating compatibility with the pictures' focal points. Choose two or three colors you want to mix together. Control your urge to add a million colors until you have created the general layout with the pictures and can determine what could be added without creating too much of a distraction.

- Do not feel that you have to match the colors that are standard for certain holidays to the pictures from that occasion. They may not be the right color for your pictures. Break away from the rules and add colors that create the feeling of the moment.

- Live in an appropriate color time for your photos. Color is your tool to create pages that tell your family history and show your personality.

Looking at these photos, you can see the effect that a different colored background can have on your focus. Notice the red background draws your eye to the barn—which is not the focus of the photo. On the other hand, the blue is more soothing and allows your eye to focus on the photo as a whole.

- Remember, color is feeling. Choose colors that create a feeling representative of the event. Allow color to recreate the fun of an occasion.

- Don't get caught in the trap of using the same colors every time. Each page should be as diverse as the memory itself. When possible, purchase paper by the sheet rather than in jumbo packages of few colors. This will give you the variety needed to add to your pages.

- Keep your paper organized, storing colors and patterns together. That way, once you realize the color that will create the mood you are looking to express, you can find all the options from your paper collection quickly and easily. Colored paper, pattern or solid, is the cheapest and easiest form of adding personality to your layout. If you are unable to buy ahead and have a variety of papers on hand, take your photos with you when you shop for paper so you can better choose the colors that will enhance your pictures.

- Place your photos against different colors to see which shades best enhance the focal point of your photo. Make sure the color you choose is not drawing your eye to something distracting in the background of the photo.

color your world

Color beckons us to open our eyes and hearts to our past. It will help us recall the beautiful moments of life that we all long to remember. It will create a mood, soothe and stimulate the brain, and make us feel wonderful in many different ways. It will color your world in a way that can have long-lasting effects, enhancing your most beautiful memories with your family. Don't be afraid to express yourself, trying different colors throughout your scrapbook. In no time, you'll be enhancing your layouts with the color that will keep your memories alive!

JILL'S NOTEBOOK

Ways to be Inspired by Color

1. Organize scrapbook paper and pens by color.
2. Take a walk and NOTICE color!
3. Buy colorful containers for desk/craft room.
4. Make up color names for distinct selections (i.e., green—kiwi, mint, limeade, spring grass).
5. Doodle with markers, pencils or paint to experiment with different combinations.
6. Make color mood notes. How does it make me feel?

Frequently Asked Questions

Q: SHOULD MY BACKGROUND PAPER BE MATCHED TO THE SAME COLORS IN MY PICTURES?

A: Not necessarily. It may enhance a particular portion of the picture that may not be the focus. Instead, choose colors to enhance the theme or to focus on the subject of the photo.

Q: WHAT COLORS SHOULD I PUT WITH VINTAGE PHOTOGRAPHS?

A: Choose subdued colors, such as neutrals, jewel tones, or soft pastels. Vintage pictures should not have to compete with color for attention in a layout.

Q: MY PHOTOS HAVE CHANGED COLORS. HOW CAN I MAKE THEM LOOK BETTER?

A: Balance the color change by choosing the color on the opposite side of the color wheel. For example, if a color has too much green in it, see how colors from the red family (pink, red, burgandy, etc.) look with it. If these colors don't enhance the mood, choose more neutral shades.

Q: HOW DO I BEGIN CHOOSING THE COLORS THAT ARE BEST FOR MY PHOTOS?

A: Begin by trying the colors that are common for the focus you have chosen. Also, consider which colors look best with the subject of your photos or which ones will serve as a neutral background.

Q: MY PHOTOS ARE TOO DARK. SHOULD I USE ONLY WHITE BACKGROUND PAPER?

A: No, but definitely stay with lighter and brighter colors.

Q: I'M A LITTLE AFRAID TO CHOOSE COLORS. HOW CAN I BE SURE I DON'T OVERDO IT?

A: Try different colors with each picture to see what you like. Nothing is final until it's glued down! See which colors speak to you and convey your personality. Remember, your scrapbook is a personal history of who you are and color is a tool to display your personality.

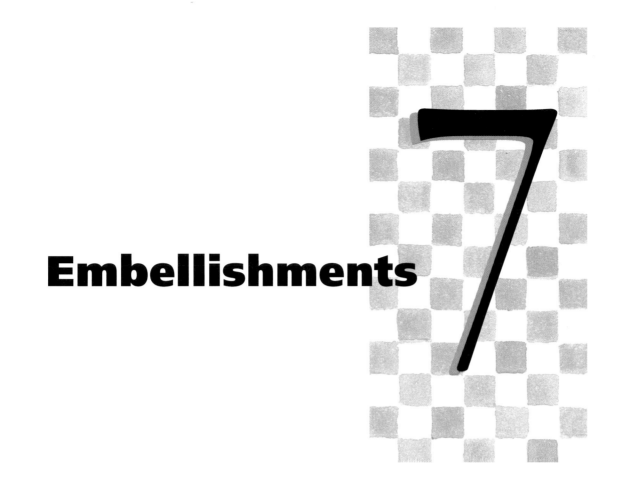

Embellishments

ALMOST EVERYONE LOOKS BETTER WITH A
little make-up; it's what adds color or interest and
enhances the beauty that was previously unnoticed. This chapter focuses on make-up for scrapbook layouts—better known as embellishing. Embellishments can enhance your photos, drawing
out the theme and focus. I will show you how decorative paper, stickers, die cuts, and other craft
tools can give that extra personality to your pages.

narrowing the scope

The most wonderful thing for any crafter living in this time, other than modern technology, of course, is the vast amount of craft supplies available to the consumer. Never have there been so many die cuts, stickers, tools, templates idea books, and types of creative paper than what is currently available. Sometimes the amount of choices can be a little overwhelming. What do I buy first? Do I need to buy everything? How can I afford it all? The good news is you don't have to have everything.

I remember a decade ago when there was barely anything for the scrapbook artist other than some colored, acid-free paper, permanent pens, and a few stickers. Those of us who were scrapbooking back then were still among the closet crafters, as scrapbooking seemed like a well-kept secret. My page layouts, although still reflecting my personality, were very different than those I make today, due to the availability and wide variety of products.

These different craft products will be your greatest tools for developing a personal style for your scrapbook pages. To make sense of it all and to help you discover which products are right for you, we will discuss the most commonly used items for scrapbook art.

paper

Paper is the most economical way to make a statement on a scrapbook page. We've come a long way since the scrapbooks from the past that only had black or white background pages. There are lightweight papers for embellishing and heavier cardstock for backgrounds and matting.

Since the eye will see a great deal of paper when viewing a scrapbook page, it is no wonder that the color and pattern choices made with paper will have a large impact on the style of the layout. In fact, paper has the capability to make or break a layout.

The color of this pattern paper, bright but subtle, accents some of the images in the photographs. The vertical lines draw the eye upward, helping to continue the theme of height that is so often seen in basketball.

This "Berry Fun" page tells the same story as the one below but something is missing. Could it be a pattern that creates a visual feast for the eye as much as strawberries are a feast for the taste buds?

There are three main types of paper used for scrapbook art: colored paper, pattern paper, and specialty paper. Each type has its own purpose and design uses. They all can be found in 8 ½" x 11" and 12" x 12", which are the industry's standard sizes.

Colored Paper

Colored paper is usually found in cardstock weight (60-80 lb. weight). You can find a variety of colors in acid-free papers that are safe for your photos. Colored cardstock paper is a staple in the scrapbook pantry. You can start by using it as the background to a layout because it's a heavier weight paper, but its usefulness does not stop there. The possibilities are endless. Use it to mat your photos (single, double, or even triple layers with contrasting colors) to give them extra attention,

Notice the difference between these two pages. This page just looks more fun than the previous one. After all, it wasn't just fun, it was "Berry Fun"!

Summer 1992

In the summer of 1992, while living in Poway, California, the kids had their first gardening experience with a few strawberries in a terra cotta pot. They were very proud of their harvest and enjoyed eating them, even though they weren't very bountiful.

cut out shapes using craft punches or scissors for decoration or journaling, make titles and borders, and much, much more!

Pattern Paper

Most pattern paper is lightweight, but there are some companies that make it in cardstock weight also. Pattern paper can be found in millions of different patterns, from basic prints, such as plaids, stripes, or dots, to more complex and busy patterns. When choosing pattern paper for a layout, remember to take into account the scale of the pattern and how many photos you plan to have on the page. If you will be placing many photos on a single page and not much of the background will be visible, then choose a small scale pattern so that the pattern will be visible. Stay away from patterns that are too busy, especially with older

photographs. Choosing patterns that are too busy for your photos will distract your eye and cause it to wander away from its focus (the photos).

Specialty Paper

This can make a scrapbook page something really special, as the look is usually very elegant and artsy. Be sure to keep in mind the acid-free concerns and test your paper with an acid-free testing pen or make sure you are buying from a store you trust. Also, some of the beautiful papers that can make a scrapbook layout really extraordinary are see-through vellums, mulberry papers with fine textures and threads, handmade papers (beware of anything too bulky), and metallic papers. Specialty papers are wonderful for wedding or heritage albums. They lend a certain sophistication that these two subjects require.

Do's and Don'ts

• **Do** choose simple pattern papers for your layout background.
• **Don't** choose anything that has colors or patterns that will compete or detract from your photos.
• **Do** buy more than one sheet of paper at a time. Dye lots vary and you may not be able to find the exact match when you need it.

Theresa I. Wolfe & Melvin J. Andraszczyk
From This Day Forward
July 18, 1953

Layouts with older photographs require a simplicity that will not overpower a black and white image. Specialty paper is used as a mat for this wedding photo, coupled with beautiful yet simple stickers.

Also, I always buy paper in pairs for possible double-page layouts.

• **Do** shop with your photos when choosing your paper, especially if you are unable to keep a varied supply at home to have in case of a scrapbook emergency! Otherwise you should stock up on a variety of colors and patterns.

• **Don't** buy a paper just because you saw it in a sample somewhere. It may never match your photos.

• **Don't** pass over a pattern paper you love just because it's not the size of your scrapbook. Larger sizes of paper can always be cut down to fit and smaller sizes can be used for accents in larger layouts.

• **Do** save all your paper scraps. Trust me, there is always something you can use them for later!

Storage Tips

Storage always depends upon how expansive your collection has become. It's also essential to keep your paper in mint condition while it is waiting to be used. You will be less likely to use paper that becomes damaged or ruined—making it useless to store it in the first place. For easy reference, it's best to keep your paper color coded. For smaller collections, keep all your paper categorized by color in file folders for easy access. I will admit I am an organization freak and get a genuine thrill out of having file folders that are the same color as the paper inside. Of course, they are also much easier to access if they are organized. As your collection grows, so will the file folders—and they can then be separated into patterns within their color subheading. Of course, all of this organization will be pointless unless your paper is stored within easy access and in a protected place, such as a file box or cabinet. If you are really into being organized, keep a color file folder for scraps too.

Knowing When Enough is Enough

Finding the proper balance with embellishing is important for keeping the focus of your pages where it belongs—on your photos. Too many decorations will cause your eye to lose focus. A good rule of thumb to remember when using different types of embellishments is:

• Two is good for you,
• Three is much to see,
• And four is really poor!

This means that two types of embellishments, such as pattern paper and die cuts are enough to add personality to your page. With the addition of a third, the background may take over and become center stage. Beyond that, your page has simply become a storage space for craft supplies. Will someone look at your scrapbook and think "is this a sticker album with photos" or "a photo album with stickers"?

Hooray for stickers and hooray for little girls! Not only are stickers quick and easy for making a page, but here they emphasize the youth and fun that is a part of this memory.

stickers

Do not think that stickers are just for kids, or even just for "cutesy" projects. If you do, then you haven't seen the stickers of today. Stickers can be found not only in fun and cute images, but elegant and classy ones as well. The companies that are truly dedicated to supplying the scrapbook artist with stickers as art can provide you with many ideas for borders, frames, alphabets and pre-made titles, and many images that can become a work of art. (Check the resource guide in the back of this book for company listings for scrapbook-safe stickers.) Stickers are safe for your scrapbook when they are acid-free, but they should not be placed directly onto a photo.

Stickers are not just cute and for kids only! Stickers can be quite elegant and pretty. Coupled with matching pattern paper made by the same company, these stickers bring a delightful look to one single, important photograph.

Stickers are sometimes sold as working components where various images are sized to work together and create scenes and action. Single layouts will look their best when you use stickers from one manufacturer because of their similarity of style, color, and design. This will guarantee that the color values and themes match and are working together to create a visual feast that is pleasing to the eye. Warning: because stickers are addicting, proceed with caution. Do not over sticker. A sticker should have a purpose and should match the scale of other embellishments being used. Allow your stickers to create a supportive focal point that is secondary to that in your photographs.

Sticker art can best be aided by the right tools. Needle nose tweezers, small sharp scissors, and a craft knife will be invaluable tools for handling, altering and designing with stickers. Keep on hand a small container of talcum powder to neutralize the adhesive in spots where it is not needed.

Do's and Don'ts

- **Don't** be afraid to alter a sticker to fit your needs. Keep it attached to its paper backing while cutting for ease in handling.
- **Do** buy stickers from a reputable company who makes stickers that are acid-free and meant for paper art.
- **Do** buy multiples of a sticker when you see it. I hate being without the perfect sticker when I need it and I know I've seen it somewhere before.
- **Don't** place stickers directly on top of photos, especially older photos!
- **Don't** think there isn't a sticker that is elegant enough for your project. Shop around and you will

be surprised at what you can find to make those special layouts look great!

- **Don't** be afraid to write on stickers with a permanent marking pen. This is a great way to add the little bits of needed information, such as the who, what, where or when of an event.
- **Do** not rub stickers into place when designing a layout. Place them delicately in place until the entire layout design has been finished. This will allow you to move them easily if you change your mind. Once you are sure of correct placement, then go back and rub them down into place.

Storage Tips

It is important that stickers be stored properly or they may be easily damaged.

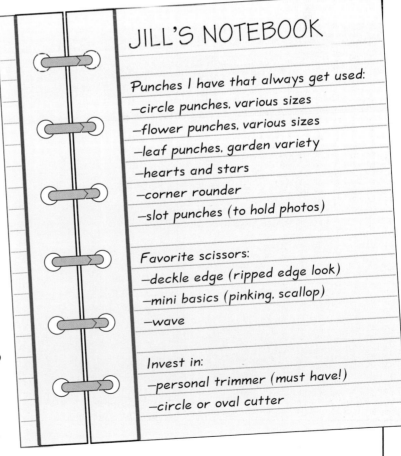

JILL'S NOTEBOOK

Punches I have that always get used:
—circle punches, various sizes
—flower punches, various sizes
—leaf punches, garden variety
—hearts and stars
—corner rounder
—slot punches (to hold photos)

Favorite scissors:
—deckle edge (ripped edge look)
—mini basics (pinking, scallop)
—wave

Invest in:
—personal trimmer (must have!)
—circle or oval cutter

In comparison to the photos, these oversized leaf die cuts give the same feeling that was felt in a playground made of giant objects. Die cuts have the power to add visual excitement to any layout.

Once again, storage options will depend upon your collection. Consider an accordion file, a coupon saver, or sticker box. When your collection grows, purchase PVC-free pocket protector sheets, such as those used for sports trading cards, slides, or photographs. Sizes will vary and can accommodate an entire collection, nicely organized in a binder format. The clear protector cover sheets allow for safekeeping and easy identification.

die cuts

Die cuts are shapes cut from paper by a machine that holds a plate with a blade that is curved into a

This paper doll beauty not only looks good on the page, but she's able to tell what the event was about. With a few added embellishments to this paper doll die cut, she looks as if she was real enough to attend the festival, too!

particular shape. Now I realize that didn't sound too exciting, but it's what you do with that shape after you have it that's exciting! Die cuts can be embellished with other elements, such as stickers, punched shapes, pattern paper and much more. Two or more die cuts can be placed together to form a completely different paper replication of a desired item. The key is to layer your die cuts with various colors so they look more realistic.

Die cuts come in many shapes. They can be alphabet letters that can be placed as titles. The shapes can also be used for journaling and other captions. At a glance, die-cut shapes can accentuate the theme chosen for your layout. Die cuts are always affordable because they are simply made from paper. They are often sold in packages or can be cut when a machine is available. Most scrapbook stores, craft stores, or schools have the machines and dies. Inquire in your area.

Do's and Don'ts

- **Do** notice that there is a wrong and right side to a die cut. The edges curve down on the right side.
- **Don't** use your die cuts as only an accent. Use them as frames and journal boxes as well.
- **Do** keep your supply organized so they are kept in good condition. If a die cut is accidentally creased, you should be able to smooth it out when you glue it down onto a page.
- **Do** buy die cuts in different colors. If you are missing the proper color for a layout, use the die cut as a pattern and trace another that will match.
- **Do** utilize your other scrapbook tools to embellish your die cuts, such as stickers, punches, markers and additional paper scraps.
- **Do** think of the 3-D object the die cut is representing and use it as a guide to add

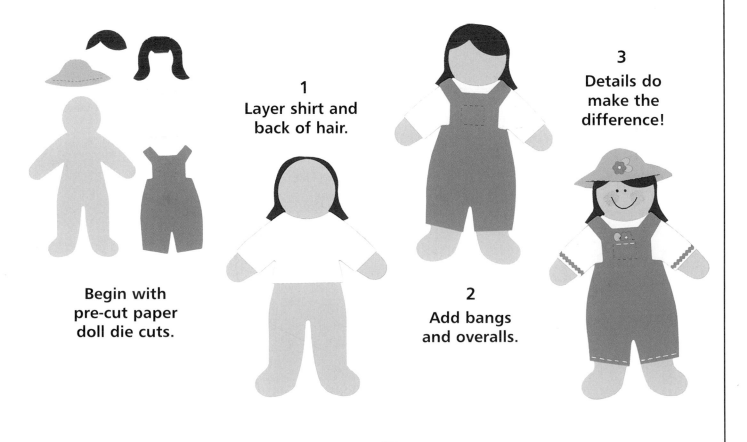

Begin with pre-cut paper doll die cuts.

1 Layer shirt and back of hair.

2 Add bangs and overalls.

3 Details do make the difference!

The kids love to jump on the trampoline!

Templates used for the letters and paper doll die cuts give allowance to "jump" right in and embellish those layouts to add personality. Embellishments should always enhance the theme of the photographs.

templates

Templates, better known as stencils, can provide you with just the right shape to embellish different elements of a scrapbook page. They are generally made of thin plastic or mylar and come in many different sizes and shapes. There are templates that can be used as journaling guides, shapes to decorate your pages, alphabets to trace and cut for titles, borders, and much more. Templates take the guesswork out of drawing and allow you to execute a more professional look in the process. When using templates as a guide to cut an image into a shape, whether on paper or on photos, trace the shape onto the back of the item with the template reversed. That way, when it is turned over to the right side, all your guidelines will be on the back side of the image. Templates, mostly alphabets or borders, can also be used right side up and traced directly onto a scrapbook layout. I recommend first using a pencil when tracing templates this way. After you finish tracing, remove the template and then go back over the markings with your permanent markers. Following this process allows mistakes to be eliminated or at least limited.

dimension to your die cut with contrasting colors and embellishing.

Storage Tips

Die cuts can be kept in different storage facilities depending on the size of the die cut. Most die cuts are about the size of an index card, so a recipe card file works great for a small collection. Die cuts are best stored by subject, such as beach, sports, school, baby, etc. That way you can refer to the subject you are scrapbooking and view all the options available to you from your current collection. When your collection has expanded beyond the size of a recipe box, consider using a large drawer or file. Don't make your storage option too big as die cuts can be damaged if there is too much movement. Envelopes work nicely for this task.

Pattern paper, alphabet templates, and a slot punch (used on the corner of the photo mat to provide a slit where the photo is inserted) create a perfect backdrop for the sweet serenity found in the face of this young boy!

Do's and Don'ts

- **Don't** cut photos into a shape that is too busy. Lay the template on top of the picture, checking to make sure that all of the elements of the photo that are important and need to be viewed fit within the design.
- **Do** invest in basic templates, such as circles, ovals, hearts, and full-bodied shapes that could accommodate a photograph.
- **Don't** trace with ball point pen on your photos unless you cut on the inside of the line, removing the pen markings in the process.
- **Do** use your templates for various purposes, such as journaling and titles.
- **Don't** cut every picture that is placed onto a single layout. There should be variety and simplicity to the shape of the photos.
- **Do** choose a shape that matches the theme you have chosen for your layout.

Storage Tips

Templates can be stored in a 3-ring binder. Some come with holes already punched for this purpose. Place a sheet of heavyweight cardstock behind each one to separate and protect them. You will also be able to see the pattern of the tem-

DO

DON'T

Joe's first attempt at playing soccer was in May 1989. It was an indoor arena in Poway, California where we lived. Most of the time the kids spent kicking each other, rather than the soccer ball. But, he had a great time playing. Good thing, since they didn't win very many games!

The grass die cut on this soccer page was crimped to add texture—just like real grass. The large soccer ball began as a die cut that was cut apart and used as a template for the pictures.

plate much quicker while flipping through your notebook. Since alphabet templates have so many areas cut out and can catch on other items, they are best kept inside a protective pocket sheet or their own file folders. The key is to keep them accessible for frequent use.

additional tools

Paper Crimper

Think of ridged potato chips and you're on the right track. A paper crimper will make ripples in your paper that can be used to add texture to die cuts and other shapes. Heavier paper works best and can even be pulled apart after crimping to remove some slight bulk without ruining the crimped look. Paper can also be

folded before being inserted into the crimper and when opened displays a unique crimped effect going in opposite directions.

Craft Knife

This handy tool can be dangerous if not used properly, but in the right hands, it can help you cut into tiny areas that are inaccessible with scissors. Use a quality self-healing mat underneath to protect your work surface. Press the tip of the craft knife into the mat and carefully maneuver it around the area to be trimmed. A craft knife is an excellent tool for silhouetting photos, picking up tiny pieces punched out from a craft punch, placing stickers into position, and many more uses. It is actually easier and safer to use when you have a sharp blade, so purchase refill blades as well.

Craft Punches

Versatility is the name of the game with punches. Craft punches come in many designs, including decorative corners, slot corners

Allow your embellishments to play a supporting role to the magic in your pictures. Alphabet letters cut from a template, sparkling tiny star stickers, and craft punches all echo the theme of this main attraction.

(that can hold a picture), borders, and much more. They come with handles for squeezing or buttons for pushing. Either way, the paper is inserted into the punch, the punch is pressed or squeezed, and out pops a shaped piece of paper—a die cut. It is like having a tiny die cut machine right in your hand! The possibilities are endless, and you are only limited by your own imagination.

Creative Edge Scissors

These scissors are found in a large variety of edges that can cut your paper into a number of interesting designs. Remember what we discussed earlier—these scissors are wonderful but are best kept for borders, mats and other decorations, not for use on your photo's edge. To obtain a

professional look, it is important to match the repeat pattern of the scissors. If necessary, draw a pencil line as a guide to help you keep on the straight and narrow. When closing the scissors, stop short of clamping all the way down and completely finishing the cut, then reposition the scissors to match the pattern on the blade and continue cutting.

Personal Trimmer

This is the one tool I could not live without. It is indispensable for making straight edges when cropping photos or paper, or adding embellishments to die cuts or background pages. Since there are several different types available, it is best to choose one that has a changeable blade. When the blade gets dull it will begin to tear your photos or paper, so it is important to have one that allows you to replace a dull blade.

READY, SET, EMBELLISH

Nine layout pages is a lot to make for just one event! However, carefully chosen embellishments that support the focus of the layout will tie them all together and keep you turning pages for the rest of the story. Page 1 starts out with die cuts and pattern paper. Pages 2 and 3 add stickers to the fun. Notice how the thin checkerboard border sticker keeps your eye moving across the layout. Pages 4 and 5 add alphabet and caption stickers. The final four pages continue the embellishments that were used in the first part of the layout and provide a great finish!

Circle or Oval Cutter

Are you searching for perfection? Now you can obtain it in at least one portion of your life. A circle or oval cutter will cut perfect circles or ovals in an instant. There are different brands on the market today but each one will cut circles or ovals ranging in size from 1" to 8", depending on the manufacturer. These must also be used with a self-healing cutting mat.

Computer Clip Art and Fonts

The age of the computer has made life easier for many reasons, and this is definitely one of them. Using your computer to word process long, detailed stories can be the difference between having that memory preserved or not. Computer fonts and clip art for frames, borders, or decoration can bring ease and simplicity to the scrapbooking adventure.

Here are a few guidelines for using these additional tools:

- **Don't** have your computer replace your own handwriting in your scrapbook. Your ancestors will want to see something written in your own hand. Balance the two, working them to your advantage.

- **Don't** use creative-edge scissors to cut the edge of your photos as it distorts the images in your photo and distracts the eye.
- **Keep** all your tools organized and away from little hands, especially knives and trimmers.
- **Keep** some wax paper handy in case you end up with a craft punch that sticks. Punch the wax paper a few times to loosen it up, or place the punch in the freezer for a short time. The more you use your punches, the easier they will be to operate.

defining your needs

Once you begin scrapbooking and come to discover your own personal style, you will see which embellishment products you are drawn to. I love to use paper, punches, and die cuts, so this is what I search for when shopping. It is often easy to get sidetracked with many new products available, but stay focused on the types you are drawn to and expand your collection of the items that you use the most. You will discover that your pages will remain a reflection of you, and your time spent scrapbooking will be a treat because you are working with what you love!

Frequently Asked Questions

Q: DOES EVERY PAGE NEED TO BE DECORATED?

A: No, but you usually find it visually more pleasing when it is. Your scrapbook layouts are more exciting with some sort of embellishing, even if it is only solid colored paper as a background. In addition, every page should not be overdecorated either. This can be too much to look at and takes up too much time! As a rule of thumb, I like to make each title page (for layouts of one event longer than 2 pages) very special, with the additional pages following in the theme more basic. With all the great products on the market today, decorating your pages is easy!

Q: I FEEL LIKE I NEED A COURSE IN SCISSOR USE 101. DO YOU HAVE ANY TIPS YOU CAN PASS ALONG?

A: How you use your scissors can make the difference between a page that looks neat or one that looks sloppy. There are a few things to remember that can help. First, when using creative-edge scissors, always take care to match up the pattern as close as possible. Second, when cutting a shape, open your scissors as wide as is comfortable to start and as you close them (smooth, no chopping action), move the paper with your opposite hand instead of moving your scissors. The line will flow easier. Also, don't clamp your scissors completely closed during continuous cutting.

Q: I LOVE STICKERS AND WANT TO USE THEM ALL THE TIME TO EMBELLISH! ARE THERE GUIDELINES TO FOLLOW SO THEY DON'T OVERPOWER MY PAGES?

A: I love stickers but you are right to be concerned. You wouldn't want someone to look at your photo album and wonder if it was a sticker album instead. First and obviously, make sure the stickers have something to do with the theme and feeling of your page. Second, consider being faithful to one sticker company throughout one book, as some companies sticker components are meant to work together. The color values and quality are the same, thereby giving a some-what uniform throughout your pages. Seek to embellish your pages while allowing your photos to remain center stage.

Q: I FEEL LIKE ALL MY PAGES LOOK THE SAME. I'M IN AN EMBELLISHING RUT. HOW DO I GET OUT?

A: There is nothing wrong with having your pages looking similar, they are a reflection of you. Don't be afraid to try something different. Start with pattern paper or try die cut art and add a little theme embellishing. The key is not to change too drastically from what you normally do.

Finding Inspiration

ALL CREATIVITY IS BASED ON TRIAL AND error. I often hear people say, "But I'm not creative." I never believe this. We can all be creative if we can learn how to take advantage of the inspiration that surrounds each of us. This chapter will help you discover ways to find inspiration and release those creative juices that we all possess.

finding inspiration

Albert Einstein said, "Imagination is more important than knowledge." Although I truly believe this, I also think that knowledge can help our imaginations flourish.

I have always been a list maker. Creating to-do lists is a daily task I enjoy. However, there is something else I have always done every day that never appears on my to-do list but is a "rule" that I always follow: I observe. Through observation I have increased knowledge, gained insight, and learned to build and refine my own personal style. Study. Watch. Notice. Listen. Open your mind to the world around you and you will be able to develop a personal style that can help define your art of scrapbooking more.

There are many sources that I look to for daily inspiration. The key is to actually take notice. I will share with you a few of my favorite places to find inspiration.

Nature

I love the color lesson that is given daily in nature. It doesn't matter which season it is because each season has its own color scheme, especially when the seasons are changing and the color variations are more obvious. After being born and raised in southern California and having the same weather all the time, I am inspired by the changing seasons in Michigan. Even on a gray day, I can find great

Nature can always inspire a page layout—both in design and theme. Notice how the torn paper adds variation of color and texture to mimic the canyon view.

No place gives more visual excitement than Las Vegas! Draw upon those elements, in this case the Statue of Liberty replica and a "Mirage" effect, that will make your layout unique.

ideas for contrast and shadow that might help enhance my photos. The shapes of leaves, flowers, and rocks are simple, yet inspiring. Notice colors, textures, and shapes. Allow nature's beauty to open your mind and inspire some grand ideas.

Advertisements

The advertising world has stayed up many late nights devising ways to catch your attention. Notice their efforts. Take note of the way pages are laid out with special note to shapes and the placement of objects. Titles and text are sometimes labeled in clever ways. Notice the size and style of fonts in lettering and interacting color. What mood is being portrayed? Check for balance and format.

Take notes, tear out ads, and place them into an idea file for later use.

Architecture

While traveling or even in your own town, notice the architecture on buildings, especially old ones. The detail in moldings, fences, and other features can give you wonderful inspiration for borders, mats, and backgrounds. Old photographs will look especially elegant with borders that mimic architecture from the era the photos were taken in. Tone-on-tone layering of colored papers and craft punches can be used to create these details. Look in architecture books and take photos of interesting architectural details for your idea file.

"The memory of the Cape lives in every corner of my mind, but it is the memory of the smell that keeps me returning."

LIZZY · JOE · LEXY · IAN

EVEN THE DOG IS ENTRANCED BY THE MAGIC OF THE CAPE

At the close of a perfect trip, we bid adieu to our personal paradise... until next year...

"The most visible joy can only reveal itself to us when we've transformed it, within."

Let inspiration guide you to share your deepest feelings for a meaningful memory. Just seeing this layout, with its soft colors and inspirational quote, reminds me of the magic I feel while at this special place.

Daily Tasks

The bustling motion around you can inspire pages. Turning wheels, scattered pillows, or stacked boxes can all be inspiration for a great layout. Sit in a spot in your house and actually look at the objects around you. Take notice of furniture, objects, automobiles, and structures—whatever is around you. What simplified version of these different shapes can you transform into something personal to use in your pages?

Poetry

There are many ways to "create a feeling" for a page. Because I am moved by words, poetry and quotes help generate feelings. Reading a quote will sometimes spark a memory of a feeling for me. This is when I know it will be perfect to add to a page. Holding onto the

Poetry can promote the enchanting feelings you may hold dear about a particular memory. Use relevant passages of poetry to relay those feelings to the readers of your scrapbook page.

feeling is my favorite part of preserving the memories, and through the use of poems or quotes, you can help convey the feelings of certain memories.

Signs and Billboards

"Signs, signs, everywhere a sign . . ." as goes the old song. Once again, shapes and lettering are key inspiration builders. I remember driving by an appliance store whose front window was emblazoned with the words "hot sale." The way the words were lettered was the real eye-catcher. I quickly pulled the car over and jotted down the idea for later. Take notes. The best part about observing is that it's free! Snap pictures of billboards or large signs for your idea file.

Conversation

We've all heard that kids say the darndest things, and my three angels are no exception. Write down words that are said, and you will not only preserve that priceless memory but you just might end up with a great idea for your layout.

People

Be picky about who you choose to scrapbook with. Some people are very inspiring to be around, while others can kill the feeling and put you into a creative funk. Attending "crops" and parties are great ways to get your creative juices flowing, but if you find you are coming home with not much done and without a renewed feeling, then it's best to scrapbook alone. It's always better to scrapbook solo than to have someone who is taking the life and inspiration out of you.

Music

Whenever I need true inspiration, I listen to music. Not only are titles and lyrics a great

Inspiration and the Internet

With all our modern technology, searching for information in a book seems archaic! With the Internet there is a plethora of information right at your fingertips and in the privacy of your own home. Go to a search page and for inspiration look up:

- Quotes
- Lyrics to Music
- Geographical Locations
- Points of Interest
- Genealogy/Family History
- Book Sellers (peruse subjects for title ideas)
- Scrapbooking Websites

You will find vast amounts of knowledge, lists, pictures, insights, and additional facts and fiction that you probably didn't know about. Any of these subjects can provide more than enough information you might need to add interest to your scrapbook pages.

Simple delicate lettering and a flower design are a perfect backdrop to this beautiful picture. Inspiration for the colors and patterns of this layout came from a trivet tile I have in my kitchen.

doesn't make it yours and may not be the best choice for your memory. Ask yourself questions about what you see: What is it that I like about this page? Why does it look good to me? Is it merely a unique product or tool that was used or is there thought and feeling put into it? By asking yourself questions, you can discover which elements of the layout truly inspire you.

influence, but hearing music and feeling it is all I need to get my creative juices flowing. Instrumental music coupled with nature sounds, such as a storm raging, wind blowing, rain falling, or crickets chirping, can fire my soul and bring that artistic feeling rushing to the surface. Of course, the only problem here is retrieving yourself from the trance and getting back to your supplies to work out that inspiration onto a page.

Layout Samples

I purposely list this one last because I feel that although it is great to find inspiration in others' work, there is a fine line between copying an idea and actually getting inspiration from it. Let others' work inspire you and ignite your creative soul to draw out your need to make it yours. Don't just copy. Copying an idea

Creating Your Own Personal Style

Give yourself a test. Look at a scrapbook idea magazine. What layouts appeal to you? Put a Post-it note on pages that you like. Do this while looking through several back issues of the magazine if you have them. Is there a style you are always drawn to? Is the artist the same or is it a series of many different people's work? What is the common thread? Notice the elements of each page that you like. Are they very busy? Very colorful? Simple and uncluttered? Bold and full of patterns? Check out the scale and lettering, all aspects of the layout. Define what is common among these pages and let it lead you to discovering and creating your own personal style.

The birth of a child is always a glorious event, and the colors used on these pages are an accurate representation of the happiness and joy of this event. These truly were the sweetest days as the title points out.

the seven-day plan

Now that you are on your way to gaining inspiration, you must actually put that to work for you and get started on some pages. I'm sure there are plenty of time restriction excuses you could come up with to not work on your books—in fact, I invented most of them. However, if you are reading this book, chances are that you do actually want to scrapbook. So I have come up with a 7-day plan (5-15 minutes daily, depending on how focused you are) to help you get some work done, even during those busy weeks. For those times when inspiration is flowing out of you non-stop and you need to scrapbook around the clock and ignore everyone around you, more power to you! For the rest of the time, this 7-day plan can help you focus on the inspiration around you everyday and help you put it to use.

Daydreaming is the best way to come up with ideas, so I have included some tips to help you draw out your own inspiration. This is for the busy person's schedule. If

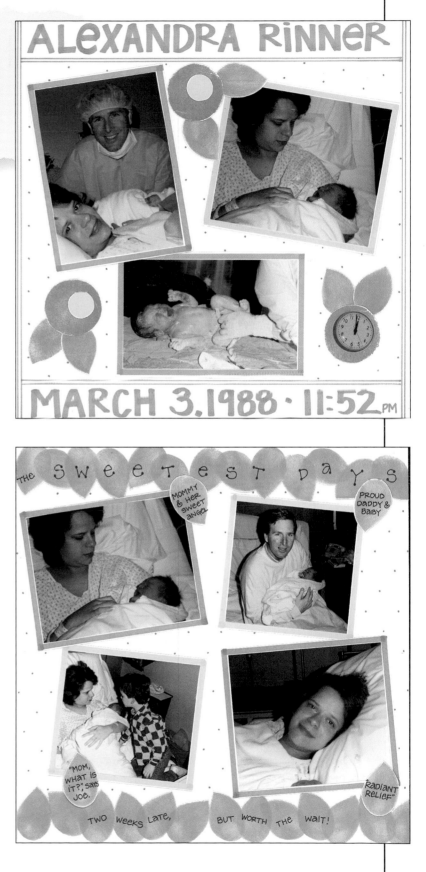

you are not busy and have all the time in the world to scrapbook, call me and I'll put you to work! For everyone else, I've developed a program to keep you inspired and motivated. And if your desire to scrapbook is very strong and you just want to work, then just get going and use the daydream tips to help keep your ideas flowing!

Day One

From your box of photos, choose an event or time period of pictures to work on. Go through the pictures and eliminate any definite rejects. With all the good ones you have left, categorize them into a timeline of that event.

DAYDREAM TIP FOR DAY 1

Start thinking about color schemes you might use. While going about your daily routine, take notice of colors and patterns around you. Make a mental note of possible color combinations for your layout.

Day Two

Choose paper, stickers, and/or diecuts that you think you may use for the layout. This might include a trip to your favorite local scrapbook store. If you have a collection of materials, peruse through it for some potential ideas. Then lay everything out on your work table so you can view it as you walk by and continue daydreaming for ideas.

Get out your supplies and move on to fabulous pages that savor your most enjoyable memories. New York is a great city for inspiration, watching people involved in all the activities that a big city provides.

Adding memorable captions to photos can help recreate the atmosphere of an activity, especially one that is as much fun as a huge toy store.

DAYDREAM TIP FOR DAY 2

While in the car today, check out shapes along the way and decide on which ones would be best to use as template shapes for cropping your pictures, if they need it. Remember, it's always best to keep the shape of your photos simple. Daydream about possible page layouts. Be sure to listen to the radio for song lyrics that could make good titles.

Day 3

Crop and trim all pictures. If you use photo squares, place them on the back of each picture. Clear off your work area and get ready for tomorrow's assembly.

DAYDREAM TIP FOR DAY 3

Notice all the letters on billboards and in magazines or newspapers. Make mental notes for ideas of possible titles for the page. Cut out samples of different font ideas for later reference.

Day 4

Mat any pictures. If you prefer to use templates to cut out your letters, trace them and carry them with so you can use that otherwise wasted time wisely. Shift your pictures around on the page to help you plan your page layout.

Creating a scrapbook page is just as much fun as the original activity. Try different shapes for your photos so not every layout looks the same.

DAYDREAM TIP FOR DAY 4

Try to recall the memory of the event. What can you remember? Casually interview other family members about the event to get their perspective.

Day 5

Affix your pictures to the page with adhesive. Write the title with creative lettering or other stickers. Leave enough room on the page for photo journaling.

DAYDREAM TIP FOR DAY 5

Think of any poems or quotes befitting the subject of your layout. Peruse quote books for inspiration, or look up quotes by subject on an Internet site.

Day 6

With your photos in place, begin the photo journaling. Who's in the pictures? When was this? Where were you? What was the occasion? Later, all this information will be extremely important to tell the story of your life. With extra space, add any embellishments desired.

The memory alone can be enough inspiration to make it easy to choose colors and shapes for your layout. I got so drenched on these rides, that large water splash shapes were an easy choice to convey the feeling of what happened!

DAYDREAM TIP FOR DAY 6

Think of which events you'd like to scrapbook next. If the weather is warm and sunny, take advantage of the inspiration around you and work on summer pages next. Or if it's really hot, get out the snow pictures and scrapbook those. All those thoughts of snowflakes are sure to cool you down!

Joe, Lizzy, Lexy and Dennis paddle downstream

AM I WET ENOUGH?!

Water Rides

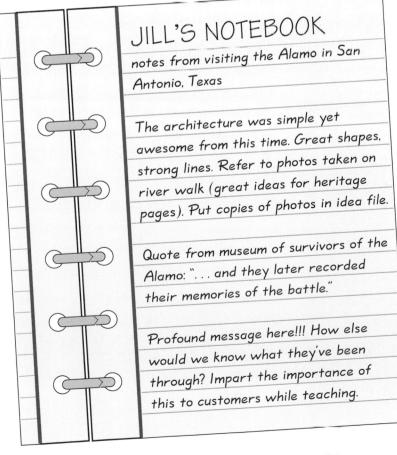

JILL'S NOTEBOOK

notes from visiting the Alamo in San Antonio, Texas

The architecture was simple yet awesome from this time. Great shapes, strong lines. Refer to photos taken on river walk (great ideas for heritage pages). Put copies of photos in idea file.

Quote from museum of survivors of the Alamo: "... and they later recorded their memories of the battle."

Profound message here!!! How else would we know what they've been through? Impart the importance of this to customers while teaching.

Day 7

After six days of great creating, there's always time for a rest. Relax and share those wonderful memories you've documented with your family. My kids love to look at their books. They feel such a sense of belonging. I really think this builds their self-esteem. Spend the day with your family creating new memories to scrapbook.

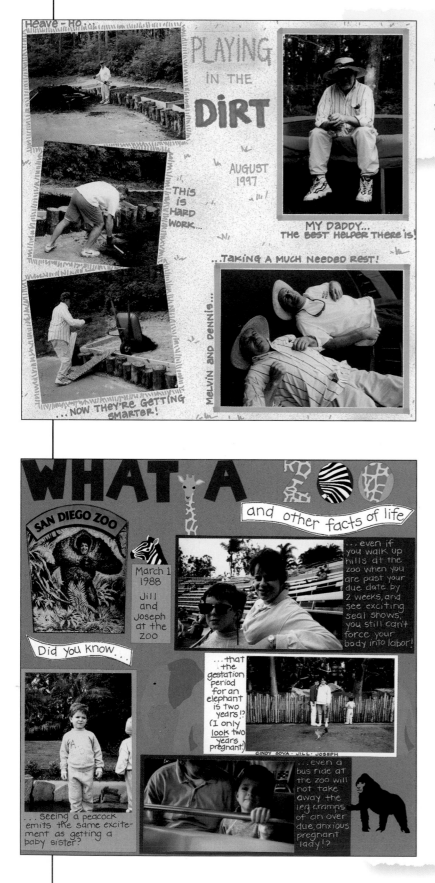

Life isn't just a series of vacations and special occasions. Simple, everyday activities can be just as memorable. Besides, the guys will always want proof of how hard they worked so they can use it for leverage later.

a note about your work space

I always feel more inspired when I have a special place to work. Cooking in a clean, beautiful kitchen is inspiring for sumptuous creations. Paper art is no different. Create a space for yourself—whether it be a closet converted to a desk space, stolen space on the dining room table, or an entire room for your art. Create a space that will inspire you. Add things that you love and that feed your soul. Include a radio for soft music, scented candles, a bulletin board plastered with things that are meaningful to you, and have all your materials organized around you.

The tidbits of animal trivia we learned while visiting the zoo were a great inspiration for this layout. They give an interesting point of view to the facts of my life at the time.

I receive much personal inspiration while visiting the Cape each year. Allow your surroundings to inspire you and recreate them on your page as part of your design.

choosing the best time for inspiration

Stop and think what makes you feel good. When are you most apt to work? In the morning before anyone wakes up, in the afternoon while the kids are busy, or late at night when the house is quiet and there are no interruptions? Set a time each day that is realistic for you. Allow yourself this time to putter for a few minutes. This should be a time for you to rejuvenate, clear your mind, and enjoy a few minutes to soak in all the morsels of inspiration you have encountered. Time is the most precious commodity we have. When putting to use the inspiration we receive daily, we can create a wonderful keepsake of memories for our families and many generations to come.

CAPE COD

The rippled sand welcomes us, year after year

OUR FAMILY

LEXY

LIZZY

JOE

As a final note, believe in your imagination and your ability to transform your world. In this way, you will be able to find the difference between your personal style and what is popular at the moment. When you bask in the daily inspiration that surrounds you, you will know that the style you have chosen is indeed "you" and that your memories will continue to live on and inspire others.

Frequently Asked Questions

Q: WHEN I SEE SCRAPBOOK LAYOUTS IN MAGAZINES AND IDEA BOOKS, I FEEL DISCOURAGED ABOUT MY OWN ABILITY. HOW CAN I GET OVER THIS?

A: Don't worry about how other people's layouts look compared to yours. Scrapbooking isn't really about art as a form as much as art as an expression. Your layouts should reflect your personality and memories. Study other layouts only for inspiration and try to notice what it is you admire about them. You may notice a few slight changes you can make to help your pages look neater and more expressive of you!

Q: I SAW A PAGE THAT I LOVE AND THAT I'D LIKE TO COPY. WHAT'S THE BEST WAY TO GO ABOUT THIS?

A: Copying someone else's idea will not give you pages that reflect your personality. Stop and notice. What is it about the layout that you liked? Shapes and layouts can be mimicked, but what about the colors that are used? Do they match your photos and the focus you have chosen? Do you even have access to the same embellishments or can you find something that would match your theme more effectively? Pull out the elements of the design that you admire, but make it your own.

Q: I GET STUMPED FOR IDEAS AND FEEL LIKE I CAN'T GET STARTED. HOW DO I GET PAST THIS CREATIVE ROAD BLOCK?

A: This is the best reason to keep an idea file. Reviewing the ideas you've admired may be just what you need to spark an idea. Start by studying your photos for clues to choosing a focus. With a few thoughts in mind, peruse your idea file or notebook for inspiration that would relate to your theme.

Q: WHAT SHOULD I USE FOR AN IDEA FILE?

A: A notebook with plenty of top loading protective sheets works great for storing ideas. It is also easy to flip through for quick inspiration. A card catalog system works nicely too (such as a recipe card file box) where you could categorize sections by subject and file ideas and cross references to other materials. A recipe card box can also be used as a means to cross reference additional ideas you may want to refer to. Categorize cards by subject and list where to locate ideas in other formats (magazines, newspapers, books, etc.).

Resources

**Chapter openers &
page numbers**
  Check pattern paper: Provo Craft

Chapter 1
Seven Peaks
  Computer font: Inspire Graphics
  Markers: EK Success

Our Little Princess
  Die cuts: Ellison
  Markers: Pantone

Lizzy's Two
  Balloon punch: Family Treasures
  Stickers: Mrs. Grossman
  Computer clip art and font: DJ Inkers
  Scissors: Fiskars
  Photo frame card: unknown

Joe's First Official Haircut
  Pattern paper: NRN Designs
  Die cut: Ellison
  Font: DJ Inkers
  Memory pocket: 3L

Our New Puppy
  Pattern paper: Design Originals
  Font: Inspire Graphics

First Day of School
  Pattern paper: Paper Patch
  Font: Inspire Graphics
  Opaque marker: EK Success
  Punch: Marvy Uchida

An Escape to the Cape
  Stripe pattern paper: Fitzgraphics
  Check pattern paper: Frances Meyer
  Doll die cuts: Jill A. Rinner designs for
    Accu-Cut
  Font: Inspire Graphics
  Alphabet template: Pebbles
  Punches: Marvy Uchida, McGill

A Day in Provincetown
  Computer clipart: DJ Inkers

Herd there was a Party
  Airbrush tool: EK Success

A Splendid Journey
  Floral paper: Frances Meyer
  Check paper: Pixie Press
  Striped paper: Stampin' Up
  Alphabet template: Pebbles

Chapter 2
Our Little Tiger Arrives
  Paper: NRN Designs
  Die cuts: Accu-Cut

Lizzy's Art Party
  Paper: Frances Meyer, NRN Designs
  Alphabet templates: Pebbles
  Die cuts: Pebbles, Accu-Cut, Ellison
  Stickers: Stickopotamus, Bernard J. Putt,
    Gick
  Computer font: DJ Inkners

Alpine Slide
  Alphabet template: Pebbles
  Font: Inspire Graphics
  Markers: EK Success

Adventureland
  Paper: Provo Craft, MPR Paperbilities
  Alphabet template: Pebbles
  Stickers: Bernard J. Putt

A Mooey Christmas
  Paper: Paper Patch
  Cow print: own design
  Alphabet template: Pebbles
  Stickers: Bernard J. Putt
  Font: DJ Inkers

Pool Fun
  Scissors: Family Treasures
  Alphabet template: Pebbles
  Stickers: Frances Meyer

  Font: Inspire Graphics
  White marker: Marvy Uchida
  Die cuts: Ellison

Party layout
  Paper: Paper Patch
  Font: Inspire Graphics

Guest list party page
  Font: DJ Inkers
  Scissors: Fiskars
  Balloon punch: Family Treasures

Slam It!
  Alphabet template: Pebbles
  Paper: Paper Patch
  Marker: Marvy Uchida

Cape Cod Bay
  Markers: EK Success
  Pattern paper: Pixie Press
  Handmade paper: Printworks

Indiana Jones
  Die cuts: Accu-Cut, Ellison
  Markers: Marvy Uchida

Hello Doctor, Goodbye Cancer
  Paper: Paper Patch, Frances Meyer
  Die cuts: Ellison, Pebbles
  Stickers: Mrs. Grossman, Bernard J.
    Putt
  ABC stickers: Sticklers
  Font: Inspire Graphics

Chapter 3
Utah on a Whim
  Alphabet template: Pebbles
  Die cuts: Ellison
  Punch: Marvy Uchida
  Font: Inspire Graphics

I Scream
  Paper: Frances Meyer
  Alphabet template: Pebbles
  Font: Inspire Graphics
  Die cut: Ellison

Punch: Marvy, McGill
Crimper: Fiskars

What We Like To Do . . .
Computer clip art: DJ Inkers

Hangin' with Friends
Doll die cut: Jill A. Rinner designs for
   Accu-Cut
Paper: Frances Meyer
Punch: All Night Media
Markers: Marvy
Font: Inspire Graphics

There's Nothing Scarier
Alphabet template: Pebbles
Scissors: Fiskars
Die cuts: Ellison, Accu-Cut

Top Ten Reasons Why . . .
Paper: Frances Meyer
Scissors: Fiskars

It Takes Two
Alphabet stamps: Stampin' Up
Markers: EK Success

We Just Want to Re . . .
Paper: Frances Meyer
Font: Inspire Graphics
Punches: Marvy

There's Plenty to Do at Epcot
Paper: Frances Meyer, Paper Patch
Die cuts: Accu-Cut, Ellison
Punches: Family Treasures
Markers: Marvy

Our First Stop
Car and signs: own design
Scissors: Fiskars
Font: Inspire Graphics
Pens: Marvy Uchida

Chapter 4
Easter Fun Hunt
Stickers: Gick
Paper: NRN Designs
Pens: EK Success

Another Year Older and Better
Stickers: Printworks
Pens: EK Success

**Pens used throughout lettering
samples**
   Marvy, EK Success

Chapter 5
Lizzy Future Olympian
Paper: Paper Patch
Star: own design
Alphabet template: Pebbles

Holy Cow
Scissors: Fiskars
Font: DJ Inkers

Our First Winter
Die cuts: Accu-Cut
Punches: Marvy, Stampin' Up

A Hole in 8
Paper: Paper Patch
Die cuts: Pebbles
Alphabet template: Pebbles
Markers: Marvy

Let the Music Begin
Die cuts: Ellison

Timberr
Die cuts: Accu-Cut, Pebbles
Alphabet templates: Pebbles

There's No Fun . . .
Paper: Paper Patch
Punch: Family Treasures
Alphabet template: Pebbles
Pens: EK Success

Waiting for Spring
Paper: Stampin' Up
Stickers: Printworks

Bahamas
Paper: Paper Patch, Memory Press,
   NRN Designs
Die cuts: Pebbles, Accu-Cut, Ellison
Alphabet stickers: Making Memories
Photo frame card: Kristin Elliot
Stickers: Frances Meyer, Bernard J. Putt
Font: Inspire Graphics

Pilgrim Monument
Alphabet template: Pebbles
Paper: Frances Meyer

Font: Inspire Graphics

Chapter 6
Florida
Alphabet template: Pebbles
Paper: Paper Patch
Die cut: Ellison
Sticker: Mrs. Grossman

Hard Rock Cafe
Paper: Paper Patch
Alphabet template: Pebbles

Disney World
Paper: Paper Patch
Alphabet template: Pebbles
Stickers: Sandy Lion, Bernard J. Putt
Punches: Family Treasures

Island Park
Die cuts: Accu-Cut
Scissors: Fiskars
Alphabet template: Pebbles

Picture in meadow
Corner punch: McGill

Child sleeping
Stickers: Mrs. Grossman

Girls on beach
Scissors: Family Treasures

Science Project
Paper: Stampin' Up
Die cuts: Ellison
Doll die cut: Jill A. Rinner designs for
   Accu-Cut
Number template: Pebbles

Sisters
Paper: Paper Patch
Scissors: Family Treasures
Alphabet template: Pebbles

Disney
Paper: MPR Paperbilities
Die cuts: Ellison
Punch: Family Treasures
Pens: Marvy

Chapter 7

Basketball Hall of Fame
Paper: Printworks
Die cut: Accu-Cut

Berry Fun
Paper: Paper Patch
Punches: Family Treasures
Die cut: Ellison
ABC die cuts: Accu-Cut

From This Day Forward
Stickers: Mrs. Grossman
Handmade paper: Printworks

Hooray for Girls
Stickers: me and my big ideas

Four Generations
Paper and stickers: Printworks

Honey I Shrunk . . .
Die cuts: Ellison
Stickers: Mrs. Grossman

Michigan Festival
Paper: Paper Adventures
Doll die cuts: Jill A. Rinner designs for
    Accu-Cut
Caption box die cut: Ellison
Stickers: Printworks
Scissors: Fiskars
Punches: All Night Media, McGill, Marvy

Paper Dolls Samples
Die cuts: Jill A. Rinner designs for Accu-
    Cut
Flower punch: All Night Media
Tear drop punch: McGill
Scissors: Fiskars

Jump
Paper: Frances Meyer, Paper Patch
Alphabet templates: Pebbles
Doll die cuts: Jill A. Rinner designs for
    Accu-Cut

Joseph 1988
Paper: Printworks
Corner slot punch: Family Treasures
Alphabet templates: Pebbles

Soccer 89
Die cuts: Accu-Cut
Paper: Paper Patch
Crimper: Fiskars
Font: Inspire Graphics
Alphabet template: Pebbles

MGM
Stickers: Mrs. Grossman
Mickey punch: Rubber Stampede
Corner punch: Family Treasures
Alphabet template: Pebbles

Picture of girls
Scissors: Fiskars

Ready, Set, Party
Paper: Paper Patch, Frances Meyer
Die cuts: Accu-Cut, Ellison
Stickers: Mrs. Grossman, Frances Meyer
Alphabet template: Pebbles
Font: Inspire Graphics

Chapter 8

Bryce Canyon
Alphabet template: Pebbles

Vegas
Die cuts: Ellison
Alphabet template: Pebbles

The Memory of the Cape . . .
Paper: Fitzgraphics
Punch: Marvy
Die cut: Ellison
Font: DJ Inkers

At the Close . . .
Paper: Paper Patch
Frame card: Kristin Elliot

Lexy
Paper: Frances Meyer
Scissors: Fiskars
Punch: Family Treasures
Alphabet template: Pebbles

Alexandra Rinner
Stamps: Printworks
Pens: Studio 2 for Printworks

On to NY City
Punches: Family Treasures
Stickers: Mrs. Grossman

Greatest Toy Store
Scissors: Fiskars, Family Treasures
Die cuts: Ellison
Stickers: Mrs. Grossman

MGM Grand Adventures
Stickers: Mrs. Grossman, Printworks
Die cut: Accu-Cut, Ellison

Water Rides
Die cut: Accu-Cut
Alphabet templates: Pebbles

Playing in the Dirt
Air brush tool: EK Success
Pens: Studio 2 for Printworks

What a Zoo
Stickers: Mrs. Grossman
Alphabet templates: Pebbles
Pens: Marvy

Cape Cod
Shell images: Kristin Elliot
Crimper: Fiskars
Alphabet templates: Pebbles

Company Information

EK Success
P.O. Box 1141
Clifton, NJ 07014
888-270-4443
(ADHESIVES, PENS, STICKERS, AND MORE)

Family Treasures
24922 Anza Dr. Unit A
Valencia, CA 91355
800-413-2645
(PUNCHES AND MORE)

Frances Meyer
P.O. Box 3088
Savannah, GA 31402
800-372-6237
(SCRAPBOOKING SUPPLIES)

Chatterbox Inc.
P.O. Box 216
Star, ID 83669
888-272-3010
(JOURNALING TEMPLATES AND MORE)

Ellison
25862 Commercentre Drive
Lake Forest, CA 92630-8804
800-253-2238
(DIE CUTS)

Mrs. Grossman's Stickers
3810 Cypress Drive
Petaluma, CA 94954
800-457-4570
(STICKERS AND MORE)

Accu-Cut
1035 E. Dodge Street
Fremont, NE 68025
800-288-1670
(DIE CUTS)

DJ Inkers
P.O. Box 1509
Sherwood, OR 97140
800-325-4890
(COMPUTER CLIP ART AND MORE)

Pebbles
P.O. Box 489
Orem, UT 84059
888-323-7878
(SCRAPBOOKING SUPPLIES)

Paper Adventures
P.O. Box 04393
Milwaukee, WI 53204
800-727-0699
(PAPER)

Fiskars
305 84th Avenue South
Wausau, WI 54401
715-842-2091
(SCISSORS, TRIMMERS, AND MORE)

The Paper Patch
P.O. Box 414
Riverton, UT 84065
801-253-3018
(PAPER)

All Night Media
P.O. Box 10607
San Rafael, CA 94912
800-783-6733
(RUBBER STAMPS, PUNCHES, AND MORE)

Inspire Graphics
P.O. Box 935
Pleasant Grove, UT 84062
801-796-9393
(COMPUTER CLIP ART AND FONTS)

me & my BIG ideas
P.O. Box 80157
Rancho Santa Margarita, CA 92688
949-589-4607
(STICKERS)

NRN Designs
5142 Argosy Avenue
Huntington Beach, CA 92649
800-421-6958
(PAPER AND STICKERS)

Marvy Uchida
3535 Del Amo Blvd.
Torrance, CA 90503
800-541-5877
(PUNCHES, PENS, AND MORE)

Mc Gill
131 E. Prarie Street
Marengo, IL 60152
800-982-9884
(PUNCHES)

Pixie Press
P.O. Box 25002
Phoenix, AZ 85002
888-834-2883
(PAPER)

Stampin' Up
800-782-6787
(RUBBER STAMPS)

Provo Craft
285 E. 900 S.
Provo, UT 84606
800-937-7686
(SCRAPBOOKING SUPPLIES)

Printworks
1242 McCann Drive
Santa Fe Springs, CA 90670
562-906-1262
(RUBBER STAMPS AND MORE)

Making Memories
P.O. Box 1188
Centerville, UT 84014
800-286-5263
(SCRAPBOOKING SUPPLIES)

Rubber Stampede
P.O. Box 246
Berkeley, CA 94701
800-632-8386
(RUBBER STAMPS AND MORE)

Index